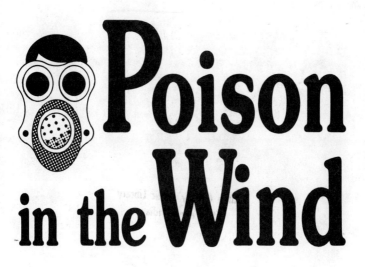

Poison in the Wind

The Spread of Chemical and Biological Weapons

Gary E. McCuen

IDEAS IN CONFLICT SERIES

502 Second Street
Hudson, Wisconsin 54016
Phone (715) 386-7113

Illustrations & Photo Credits

Carol*Simpson 112, 132, Daily World 82, Kirk 71, David Seavey 11, 93, Ron Swanson 59, 88, United States Department of Defense 17, 32, 37, 50, 119, 125, 137. Cover illustration by Ron Swanson.

©1992 by Gary E. McCuen Publications, Inc.
502 Second Street, Hudson, Wisconsin 54016

(715) 386-7113

International Standard Book Number 0-86596-084-4 Printed in the United States of America

CONTENTS

CHAPTER 3 U.S. CHEMICAL WARFARE PROGRAM IN VIETNAM: Points and Counterpoints

CHAPTER 4 THE BIOLOGICAL WEAPONS DEBATE

CHAPTER 5 HALTING THE SPREAD OF
CHEMICAL WEAPONS

REASONING SKILL DEVELOPMENT

These activities may be used as individualized study guides for students in libraries and resource centers or as discussion catalysts in small group and classroom discussions.

IDEAS in CONFLICT ®

This series features ideas in conflict on political, social, and moral issues. It presents counterpoints, debates, opinions, commentary, and analysis for use in libraries and classrooms. Each title in the series uses one or more of the following basic elements:

Introductions that present an issue overview giving historic background and/or a description of the controversy.

Counterpoints and debates carefully chosen from publications, books, and position papers on the political right and left to help librarians and teachers respond to requests that treatment of public issues be fair and balanced.

Symposiums and forums that go beyond debates that can polarize and oversimplify. These present commentary from across the political spectrum that reflect how complex issues attract many shades of opinion.

A *global* emphasis with foreign perspectives and surveys on various moral questions and political issues that will help readers to place subject matter in a less culture-bound and ethnocentric frame of reference. In an ever-shrinking and interdependent world, understanding and cooperation are essential. Many issues are global in nature and can be effectively dealt with only by common efforts and international understanding.

Reasoning skill study guides and discussion activities provide ready-made tools for helping with critical reading and evaluation of content. The guides and activities deal with one or more of the following:

RECOGNIZING AUTHOR'S POINT OF VIEW

INTERPRETING EDITORIAL CARTOONS

VALUES IN CONFLICT

WHAT IS EDITORIAL BIAS?

WHAT IS SEX BIAS?

WHAT IS POLITICAL BIAS?

WHAT IS ETHNOCENTRIC BIAS?

WHAT IS RACE BIAS?

WHAT IS RELIGIOUS BIAS?

*From across **the political spectrum** varied sources are presented for research projects and classroom discussions. Diverse opinions in the series come from magazines, newspapers, syndicated columnists, books, political speeches, foreign nations, and position papers by corporations and nonprofit institutions.*

About the Editor

Gary E. McCuen is an editor and publisher of anthologies for public libraries and curriculum materials for schools. Over the past years his publications have specialized in social, moral and political conflict. They include books, pamphlets, cassettes, tabloids, filmstrips and simulation games, many of them designed from his curriculums during 11 years of teaching junior and senior high school social studies. At present he is the editor and publisher of the *Ideas in Conflict* series and the *Editorial Forum* series.

CHAPTER 1

BIOLOGICAL WEAPONS: HISTORY AND OVERVIEW

1   BIOLOGICAL WEAPONS: HISTORY AND OVERVIEW

THE HISTORY OF BIOLOGICAL WARFARE AND RESEARCH

Victor W. Sidel

Since World War II there have been numerous allegations of biological weapons development and even use by a number of nations including the United States.

Attempts to use biological weapons have a long history. In ancient Persia, Greece and Rome, diseased corpses of men and animals were used to contaminate wells and other sources of drinking water. When the Mongols besieging the Black Sea port of Caffa began in 1347 to die of plague, the survivors catapulted the corpses into the city, and the Genoese who were defending it also began to die of plague. The defenders fled, contributing to the spread of "the black death" to Italy and indeed all of Europe. On our own continent, during the French and Native American War, Lord Jeffrey Amherst, the commander of the British forces at Fort Pitt, is said to have given blankets containing scales from victims of smallpox to the Native Americans surrounding the fort, causing, it is believed, a smallpox outbreak.

Victor Sidel is a physician with special training in internal medicine and public health. Sidel is a distinguished University Professor of Social Medicine at Monte Fiore Medical Center/Albert Einstein College of Medicine in the Bronx, New York and is past president of the American Public Health Association (APHA) and of the Physicians for Social Responsibility (PSR). This reading was excerpted from congressional testimony by Mr. Sidel before the Senate Committee on Governmental Affairs, May 17, 1989.

20th Century Applications

During the negotiations for the Geneva Protocol for the Prohibition of the Use in War of Asphyxiating, Poisonous or other Gases, and of all Analogous Liquids, Materials or Devices and of Bacteriological Methods of Warfare in 1925, the abhorrence of biological weapons was so great that "bacteriological methods" were added to what had originally been envisaged as only a chemical weapons treaty. The Protocol, to which over 100 nations are party, prohibits the use, but not the production or possession, of chemical and biological weapons in warfare. A number of nations reserve the right to respond in kind, so this is basically a "no first use" treaty.

When Japan attacked China in the 1930s, it is alleged that rice and wheat grain were mixed with fleas carrying plague, resulting in plague in areas of China that had not had plague before. Other bacteria may have also been used as weapons by Japanese troops and there are reliable reports of extensive experimentation in a Japanese biological weapons laboratory in China on the effects of these weapons on prisoners of war from a number of different countries. According to testimony at the Nuremberg trials, prisoners at German concentration camps such as Buchenwald were infected in tests of biological weapons. During World War II it is alleged that Germany infected Romanian Cavalry horses with glanders. The British are known to have released anthrax spores on Gruinard Island off the coast of Scotland; it remained uninhabitable for many years. Churchill is said to have considered attacking German livestock with anthrax, but this was never carried out. In the U.S., work on anthrax and brucellosis as weapons was performed. There have also been reports of Soviet research on biological weapons during World War II.

Since World War II there have been numerous allegations of biological weapons development and even use by a number of nations including the United States. Most of these are unsubstantiated and some of them effectively refuted. These include: the allegation by the U.S. that the "yellow rain" seen in Laos and Cambodia was a biological weapon released by the Soviets and the Vietnamese; the allegation by Secretary of Defense Weinberger that an outbreak of anthrax in the Soviet city of Sverdlovsk was "evidence of inadvertent release of anthrax bacteria from a highly secured military installation"; allegations by China and by Cuba of the introduction of biological weapons into North Korea and Cuba by the U.S.; and

the allegation by the U.S. that Iraq had been developing biological weapons agents.

Documented Use

But in some instances the facts are documented. For example, it was revealed in 1969 that in the 1950s and 1960s the University of Utah had under contract conducted secret experiments at the U.S. Army Dugway Proving Grounds involving large-scale field testing of some of the most infectious and toxic biological warfare agents including tularemia, Rocky Mountain spotted fever, plague and Q fever. This was also the site of the 1968 discharge of nerve gas which because of unexpected wind conditions killed thousands of livestock, a topic on which 20 years ago I testified before a Congressional committee. In 1950, U.S. Navy mine sweepers released aerosolized Serratia Marsescens in sufficient quantities to contaminate 117 square miles of the San Francisco area. This presumably harmless species, used as a *simulant*, a presumably non-pathogenic organism used as a stand-in for a pathogenic organism, proved to be dangerous particularly to immunologically-compromised individuals. During the 1950s and 1960s, the U.S. conducted 239 top-secret open-air disseminations of simulants involving such areas as the subways of New York City, the Kittatinny and Tuscarora tunnels on the Pennsylvania Turnpike, and Washington National Airport. So far as can be ascertained, there was no notification or attempt to gain approval for these tests from the people, the municipalities or the health authorities of the areas involved, not even to alert them to the potential danger if anything went wrong.

The 1972 Convention

In 1969 the Nixon Administration announced that the U.S. would unilaterally dismantle its biological weapons program because such weapons were militarily useless, were no threat to the U.S. or its security, and were especially repugnant because of their anti-civilian nature and uncontrollability. In 1972 the convention on the Prohibition of the Development, Prevention and Stockpiling of Bacteriological (Biological) and Toxin Weapons and on Their Destruction was concluded. It was ratified by the U.S. in 1975 (the same year in which the Senate ratified the Geneva Protocol of 1925), and over 100 nations are party to it. The Convention prohibits (except for "prophylactic, protective and other peaceful purposes") the development, production, stockpiling, transfer or acquisition of biological agents or toxins, as well as weapons and means of delivery. As we shall see, the exception creates a large potential loophole in the Convention.

Renewed Testing

In recent years, perhaps because of the spectre of new biological weapons produced by genetic engineering techniques or because of allegations of aggressive biological weapons programs in other countries, the U.S. decision to totally dismantle its biological weapons program seems at least in part to have been reversed. Funding for the U.S. Army Biological Defense Research Program (BDRP) in the U.S. has quadrupled since 1981 ($15.1 mil in 1981; $60 mil in 1988) and the basic research component of BDRP activities, including research sponsored at universities or private laboratories, increased 60-fold from 1981 to 1986. These facts may suggest to other nations that the U.S. has renewed its interest in biological weapons and to some nations may suggest potentially hostile intent.

To take a specific example, at the University of Massachusetts at Amherst, research sponsored by the BDRP has the stated purpose of developing an improved vaccine for troops stationed in developing countries where anthrax is a problem. There are indeed diseases such as malaria and typhoid, which affect millions of people and for which control measures are inadequate, on which intensive research to find methods to protect troops as well as civilians would surely be justified. But anthrax is not one of these diseases. Anthrax, in short, would seem to be of interest not because of its natural occurrence but because of its potential as a biological weapon.

Given this relatively low public health priority for the development of another anthrax vaccine, we became concerned about this research for two reasons: (1) Research of this kind inevitably poses some risk of release of virulent organisms into the environment with the danger of infection of people or animals in the surrounding community; and (2) Research of this kind inevitably contributes to escalating development, production and stockpiling of biological weapons with the danger of use of these weapons in war or terrorism or their accidental dissemination.

13

Concerns About Testing

1) Biological weapons, like chemical weapons, are largely anti-civilian weapons. Troops can often be protected, fully or partially. Civilians, particularly the very young, the old and the sick usually cannot be protected. These weapons have therefore been called "public health in reverse" and have earned the abhorrence in which they are held by all civilized people. Indeed it is for this reason that over 800 physicians and scientists have signed a pledge not to "engage in research or teaching that will further the development of chemical or biological warfare agents."

2) Any research targeted at development of defenses against biological weapons that is ambiguous enough to cause other nations to believe that an offensive capability is being developed and therefore causes them to work on biological weapons is to everyone's detriment. It merely makes the eventual use by terrorists or others more likely, with no discernible benefit.

3) If the intent of current Department of Defense (DOD) biological programs is indeed defensive, then it appears logical to hand them over to civilian agencies, with the presumption of prompt, regular reporting of all research methods and of all findings in the open scientific and medical literature, thus avoiding even the appearance of strengthening offensive capability without sacrificing the capability to defend as effectively as possible against biological weapons attacks by others.

4) Regarding a strong convention outlawing biological weapons and providing for a verification, this suggests the need for a worldwide inspection capacity under international control. Much work is required on the methods, including the needed access, for verification.

2 BIOLOGICAL WEAPONS: HISTORY AND OVERVIEW

CHARACTERISTICS OF BIOLOGICAL AND TOXIN WEAPONS

Matthew Meselson, Martin Kaplan, and Mark A. Mokulsky

Delivered by aircraft, missile, or other means and dispersed near the ground as wind-borne aerosols to be inhaled by a target population, certain infectious agents could in theory approach the anti-personnel effectiveness of thermonuclear warheads.

Infectious Agents

The development, production, stockpiling, acquisition, and transfer of biological and toxin weapons are prohibited by the Biological Weapons Convention of 1972 (the BWC), to which more than 100 states are party. Unlike the Geneva Protocol of 1925, that prohibits the use but not the possession of biological and chemical weapons, the BWC is a true disarmament treaty, in that it seeks the actual elimination of a class of weapons. Since

Matthew Meselson is Professor of Biochemistry and Molecular Biology at Harvard University. Martin Kaplan is former scientific director of the World Health Organization. Mark Mokulsky is a biophysicist in the Soviet Union. This reading was excerpted from testimony on the Verification of Biological and Toxin Weapons Disarmament before the House Subcommittee on Immigration, Refugees and International Law of the Full Committee on the Judiciary, May 1, 1990.

the BWC entered into force in 1975, its very limited confidence-building and verification provisions have been significantly augmented. This has been accomplished not by amending the Convention itself but rather through agreements among its States Parties, reached at its First and Second Review Conferences, and also through actions taken at the United Nations. Additional strengthening of the regime for verifying biological and toxin weapons disarmament is expected to result from the Third BWC Review Conference in 1991.

Biological weapons employing infectious agents pathogenic to man have the potential to kill or incapacitate populations over large areas. This potential derives from the extreme smallness of the amount of agent sufficient to initiate infection. Delivered by aircraft, missile, or other means and dispersed near the ground as wind-borne aerosols to be inhaled by a target population, certain infectious agents could in theory approach the anti-personnel effectiveness of thermonuclear warheads, in terms of the weight of the agent and associated dissemination devices required to attack a given area. Moreover, infectious agents could lend themselves to modest, perhaps even rather inconspicuous means of delivery.

Today, no nation is known to possess biological weapons. During World War II, however, Great Britain, Japan, and the United States developed biological weapons based on explosive and insect dissemination of the agents of anthrax, plague, and other diseases. The infectious anti-personnel agents stockpiled for use in weapons by the United States before its unilateral renunciation of biological weapons in 1969 included *Francisella tularensis*, the bacterium responsible for tularemia, *Coxiella burnetii*, the rickettsial organism responsible for Q fever, and VEE, the virus that causes Venezuelan equine encephalomyelitis. In addition, there were stocks of biological agents intended for use against food crops: *Pyricularia oryzae* and *Puccinia graminis*, the fungi responsible for rice blast and wheat rust, respectively. Examples of other infectious anti-personnel agents that have been studied for use in weapons or have been actually stockpiled are the viruses that cause Chikungunya fever, Eastern equine encephalomyelitis, and yellow fever; the bacteria that cause brucellosis, cholera, and glanders; and the rickettsiae responsible for Rocky Mountain spotted fever and epidemic typhus. In addition, many other naturally-occurring infectious agents may have the stability, infectivity, virulence, and other characteristics suited to use in weapons for use against people,

16

The Soviets maintain the largest Nuclear-Biological-Chemical (NBC) warfare capability in the world, including specialized troop equipment and vehicles designed to operate in a nuclear environment.

Source: United States Department of Defense

17

> ### BACTERIA THAT KILL
>
> Bacillus anthracis *or anthrax bacteria is almost 100 percent fatal when one is exposed by aerosol to approximately 8,000 spores, and death will likely occur in less than 7 days.* Francisella tularensis, *a bacteria that causes tularemia, known as rabbit fever, is highly infectious. Less than 10 organisms can cause disease with symptoms occurring in only 3 to 5 days. As many as 30 percent to 60 percent of those affected will die within 30 days if not treated.*
>
> Barry J. Erlick, Ph.D., Committee on Governmental Affairs, Feb. 9, 1989.

animals, or plants.

Contrary to a prevalent misconception, the development and production of reliable weapons based on infectious agents would be a major undertaking. Large technical resources and expenditures would be required for initial study, development, testing, and production of the biological agent itself, the devices for its dissemination, the means for their delivery, and the fully integrated biological weapon system. Even then, serious uncertainties in performance would remain. Nevertheless, such weapons could be simpler and less expensive to produce than nuclear weapons. Moreover, rudimentary but highly dangerous biological weapons of lower reliability could be produced with much less effort and expense, using widely available technology. Crude biological weapons are within the reach of many nations and even dissident groups and terrorists.

Toxins

Toxins are poisonous substances made by living things. The term is also applied to the synthetically produced analogues of such substances. Unlike infectious agents, toxins cannot reproduce. While infectious agents generally require incubation periods of a few days following exposure before illness develops, some toxins can cause incapacitation or death within minutes or hours. Examples of toxins that have been studied for use in weapons are the botulinal toxins including ricin, present in castor beans. Even humans produce substances that could in theory be used to cause poisoning leading to incapacitation or death.

Some toxins, for example tetrodotoxin, made by the globefish, have been chemically synthesized. The BWC states that its prohibitions apply to toxins regardless of their means of production.

It is for tactical battlefield use, where rapid action is an important factor, that toxins have been principally considered. For this purpose, however, the utility of toxins, including those that might be developed by genetic engineering or other new technologies, must be judged in comparison with that of already developed, weaponized, tested, and stockpiled chemical warfare agents, such as the highly lethal and rapidly-acting organophosphorus nerve agents and the blistering and blinding agent, mustard. Unlike these well-known chemical warfare agents, which are highly stable liquids of simple chemical structure, toxins are generally complex organic substances. Accordingly, they are solids and often have lower stability to withstand heat, surface forces, and oxidation. Not unexpectedly, attempts to weaponize toxins encountered serious difficulties in maintaining agent stability during and after release and in achieving efficient aerosolization. Other factors, including the difficulty of formulating toxin agents able to penetrate the skin and the expense and difficulty of manufacture also mitigated against successful development of toxin weapons.

Although considerable efforts were made to weaponize certain toxins during World War II and afterwards, no nation is known to possess toxin weapons or to have developed a battlefield weapon based on toxins that would be competitive with chemical weapons already stockpiled.

Protection Against Biological and Toxin Weapons

Under certain conditions, medical procedures such as immunization or administration of antibiotics or other drugs can offer protection against some biological agents and toxins. For immunization, adequate supplies of vaccine against the specific threat agent must be on hand in advance and sufficient time must be available for administration to the population at risk. In addition, for vaccines, a period of days to weeks must be allowed for immunity to develop. For many infectious agents and toxins no effective vaccines have been developed and, in some cases, even persistent development efforts have been unsuccessful. These severe limitations on medical means of protection against infectious agents and toxins make such protection ineffective or impractical except under certain quite restrictive conditions.

The only generally effective protection against all airborne biological agents and toxins is not medical but mechanical, namely the provision of filtered or otherwise purified air. A well-fitted military gas mask provides a high degree of protection against inhalation of infectious agents and toxins. Collective shelters and vehicles with filtered air serve the same purpose. Such equipment is already widely deployed with modern armed forces for protection against chemical warfare agents and radioactive fallout. There is as yet, however, no completely reliable equipment for rapid detection of airborne biological and toxin agents. Of course, if a sufficient degree of threat is thought to exist during a particular mission, military units could be placed in protective posture for the duration of the mission. Moreover, if chemical or biological weapons have once been used in a particular conflict, military forces are likely to be ordered into an advanced state of protection when under any form of surface or air attack.

The protection of large civilian populations would be much more difficult than the protection of military units. It would require the development and provision of reliable alarm systems, the issuance of gas masks, the construction of neighborhood and workplace shelters, the conduction of regular education and drill for the entire population, and massive preparations for medical diagnosis and care. Such a defense would be immensely expensive and stressful to create and maintain.

Of course, there is clearly merit in having fast-response epidemiological teams and limited emergency supplies of certain vaccines, antibiotics and other supplies in order to cope with natural threats to public health. Such preparations may also be able to mitigate the effects of limited acts of sabotage, depending on the agent employed. Nevertheless, protection of the civilian population against a determined large-scale biological attack would be a very large undertaking.

Clearly, the proliferation of biological weapons would constitute a grave threat to the civilian populations and economies of all states, including those of the nuclear powers. Once started, the proliferation of biological weapons could be much more difficult to arrest than that of nuclear weapons, owing to the relative simplicity and wide availability of the underlying technology. These considerations were central to the decision of the United States to renounce biological and toxin weapons unilaterally, and to the achievement of the BWC.

3 BIOLOGICAL WEAPONS: HISTORY AND OVERVIEW

CLONING ADDS A DEADLY BITE TO BIOLOGICAL WARFARE

Gary Thatcher

"Microbes are the foot soldiers of the 21st century."

In the hands of a spy or a terrorist, it's an ideal poison.

About all the victim feels is a momentary sting when the dart or pellet breaks the skin. He's unlikely to have built up natural immunity. And an antidote, while available, is fairly rare, and probably not at hand. Even if treatment is available, it's difficult to figure out just what insidious toxin is at work—perhaps until it's too late.

The substance is rattlesnake venom.

The problem is—or rather, used to be—collecting it. "Milking" snakes was a time-consuming, unpredictable and dangerous task.

For years, the United States government kept only tiny amounts of venom stockpiled for research purposes and for producing antidotes. It also was kept for "special operations" by intelligence agencies—assassinations.

But now the United States and the Soviet Union can produce nearly unlimited amounts of rattlesnake venom—by "cloning" the venom without ever going near a snake.

Gene Splicing

Cloning involves the use of recombinant DNA technology, or "gene splicing." A simple, harmless microbe—such as one that's common in the human intestine—can be altered so that as it reproduces itself, it also reproduces new genetic material that has been spliced onto it.

Cloning is a biological breakthrough that was only dawning 16 years ago, when many of the world's nations banned biological warfare. It has opened up the possibility of a new generation of chemical and biological weapons.

It also has spawned a multimillion dollar military competition, involving the deadliest microbes, viruses and bacteria known to man. It's a race to identify—and protect against—exotic new toxins and biological warfare agents.

Jeremy Rifkin, president of Washington's Foundation on Economic Trends, puts it graphically: "Microbes are the foot soldiers of the 21st century." The foundation is concerned with the moral and ethical questions of biotechnology, and has filed a number of lawsuits to limit the Pentagon's chemical and biological defense research programs.

Most of those programs are conducted openly, but the Pentagon also conducts classified research, the results of which are kept secret.

U.S. intelligence agencies say that 10 countries, including the Soviet Union, are involved in prohibited biological weapons research.

Pentagon sources say the United States is forced to spend millions of dollars annually to research the threat posed by new weapons, and to defend against them.

The Reagan years have produced something of a boom for biological defense research. The Pentagon's budget for the program rose from $15.1 million in 1981 to about $90 million in 1986.

The United States renounced offensive biological warfare in 1969, convinced the weapons were unpredictable and inhumane. It converted the biological weapons facility at Fort Detrick, Maryland, into a research center.

In 1972, the United States, the Soviet Union and other countries signed the Convention on the Prohibition of the Development, Production and Stockpiling of Bacteriological and

Toxin Weapons. The convention essentially outlawed biological warfare. It did not, however, prohibit defensive research. The United States and the Soviet Union have maintained extensive defense research programs all along.

The Pentagon acknowledges that it is creating some disease-causing substances, using such techniques as recombinant DNA research.

Some have no known antidotes. The possibility that they could be altered, even inadvertently, to make them even more deadly or harder to defend against, is troubling to the Pentagon's critics.

"We're talking about the possibility of powerful new genetic weapons that could rival nuclear weapons in the future," said Rifkin. "People think AIDS (acquired immune deficiency syndrome) is dangerous. Imagine what could happen if military establishments set out to deliberately create a virus that has no cure."

For years, the dividing line between chemical and biological warfare was clear: Biological agents could reproduce themselves. Chemical agents could not.

But U.S. and Soviet scientists say the line now is blurred by advances in biotechnology. Things that can't reproduce themselves in nature can be reproduced in a laboratory. Consequently, a "gray area" is developing between classic chemical warfare agents, such as mustard gas and nerve agents, and biological agents.

Novel Agents

Specialists have adopted a catch-all term for substances in this gray area: They call them "novel agents." Among them are:

- Well-known biological warfare agents, such as anthrax, produced by new methods, such as genetic engineering.

- Toxins, such as spider venom, previously so difficult to collect that they were discounted as warfare agents.

- Unique mixtures of poisons, resulting in compounds that are potentially more lethal, virulent or difficult to treat than the component parts.

- Substances that occur naturally in the human body, such as biological regulators and hormones, but that in abnormal amounts can have an unpredictable impact on human life.

- "Low-molecular-weight agents" — poisonous chemicals of such small proportions that they could, theoretically, slip through the activated charcoal filters of a gas mask or protective suit, as air molecules do.

- Genetically altered micro-organisms that closely resemble known disease-causing agents, but have a critical change in protein structure that renders present-day vaccines obsolete.

At present, bioengineering is producing "the same old substances," says Nikita Smidovich, a diplomat in the Soviet Foreign Ministry's Department on Peaceful Use of Outer Space and Nuclear Energy. But, he warns, "If we look into the future, there could be things that surpass the lethality of known agents."

The U.S. biological warfare defense program, when compared with that of the Soviet Union, is a model of openness. Contracts are a matter of public record, and there is extensive documentation of the research in environmental impact statements and other documents.

In addition, the Pentagon's main biological defense research facility, the U.S. Army Medical Research Institute of Infectious Diseases at Fort Detrick, issues an annual report detailing the research it is supporting.

Secret Tests

Gen. Howard Eggleston, head of the Army's Space and Special Weapons Directorate, also confirms that "there is a program that's no part of the biological defense research program at Fort Detrick."

It involves testing with simulants (microbes that mimic dangerous substances but are not themselves harmful) and novel agents. The test results are not reported publicly.

In 1988, in response to a lawsuit by the Foundation for Economic Trends, the Defense Department revealed that it is researching a veritable rouges' gallery of bacteria, viruses and toxins.

Among the substances are bacteria-like *Yersina pestic*, the "Black Death" of the 14th century, and tularemia (rabbit fever) which is known to cause blisters, high fevers, and in some cases, death.

Also on the list are virus diseases, including well-known ones such as yellow fever and polio, and rare, exotic ones with names such as Chikungunya and O'Nyong Nyong.

The Pentagon also acknowledged in the legal proceeding that it is researching the military uses of toxins from cobras, rattlesnakes, scorpions and shellfish.

These bacteria, viruses, and toxins are lethal enough in their own right. But Pentagon strategists say there is a possibility that novel agents could, in effect, combine the worst aspects of the lot—with nightmarish battlefield results.

Eggleston says the Pentagon has considered the possibility that computers, using artificial intelligence techniques, could be used to concoct formulas for such deadly potions. The Pentagon, he says, must try to anticipate such threats, and ensure that U.S. soldiers are protected.

Soviet Research

A majority of Congress repeatedly has been convinced that chemical and biological defense research is necessary. One key reason: suspicion that the Soviet Union is secretly conducting research on offensive biological warfare and beefing up its capability.

U.S. intelligence agencies say they have confirmed the existence of two Soviet facilities for biological warfare research.

The Pentagon also says there is a biological warfare test facility on Vozrozhdeniya Island in the Aral Sea.

The Soviets, in documents filed with the United Nations, said that the Ministry of Defense conducts research with various biological warfare agents at laboratories in Sverdlovsk, Zagorsk, Leningrad, Kirov and Aralsk. But the Soviet Union maintains that all the facilities are involved in defensive research only, not offensive, and certainly not in weapons production.

But Lt. Col. David Huxsoll of the U.S. Army's Medical Research Institute for Infectious Diseases says the continuing search for chemical and biological defenses is not only a question of prudence, but one of morality.

"If we have any suspicion that these things are going to be used, then I don't have a moral problem with research to protect against these potential threats," he said. "I think it would be immoral if we didn't protect against them."

INTERPRETING EDITORIAL CARTOONS

This activity may be used as an individualized study guide for students in libraries and resource centers or as a discussion catalyst in small group and classroom discussions.

Although cartoons are usually humorous, the main intent of most political cartoonists is not to entertain. Cartoons express serious social comment about important issues. Using graphic and visual arts, the cartoonist expresses opinions and attitudes. By employing an entertaining and often light-hearted visual format, cartoonists may have as much or more impact on national and world issues as editorial and syndicated columnists.

Points to Consider

1. Examine the cartoon for this activity on page 11.

2. How would you describe the message of the cartoon? Try to describe this message in one to three sentences.

3. Do you agree with the message expressed in this cartoon? Why or why not?

4. Does the cartoon support the author's point of view in any of the readings in this chapter? If the answer is yes, be specific about which reading or readings and why.

5. Are any of the readings in Chapter One in basic disagreement with this cartoon?

CHAPTER 2

CHEMICAL WEAPONS: HISTORY AND OVERVIEW

4   CHEMICAL WEAPONS: HISTORY AND OVERVIEW

CHARACTERISTICS OF CHEMICAL WARFARE AGENTS

Chemical Warfare Review Commission

The mask alone will protect against death from mustard agent; the burns are painful and temporarily disabling, but seldom fatal. Nerve agent absorbed through the skin, however, can result in death within a few minutes.

Unlike "conventional" weapons, which cause casualties by piercing or tearing apart the body, chemical weapons deliver agents that react with human tissue, chemically changing in a way that injures or kills. Like the radiation (as opposed to heat and blast) effect of nuclear weapons, they attack the physiology, rather than the external anatomy, of the body. Because they have no blast or heat, most chemical weapons damage only living organisms, leaving structures and terrain unaffected.

Chemical agents that have been developed for weapons are commonly classified according to the way in which they can be dispersed; the way they attack the body; and the length of time they remain able to attack the body. Most chemicals usable for war are not gases, although "poison gas" is a term colloquially used to refer to them. The first lethal chemical used in combat, in 1915, was the gas chlorine, and "gas" became the common term. Most agents in chemical munitions, however, are liquids, which are dispersed either as droplets or vapors.

This reading was excerpted from the June 1985 "Report of the Chemical Warfare Review Commission." The Commission was established by Congress and its presidentially appointed members included former National Security Affairs Assistant Zbigniew Brzezinski and retired Army General Alexander Haig, Jr.

Types of Agents

The chemical agents used in World War I were chlorine-based compounds, such as chlorine gas and phosgene, with the more toxic and dangerous mustard gas developed later in the war. The three significant types of known modern agents and their military letter designation are:

- Blister agents (mustard, H; Lewisite, L), which burn any body surface with which they come in contact and can kill through secondary effects of blistering in the respiratory system.

- Blood agents, (hydrogen cyanide, AC; cyanogen chloride, CK), which enter the body by the respiratory system and attack the blood cells, interfering with their ability to carry oxygen.

- Nerve agents, which include the "G" agents Tabun (GA) Sarin (GB), and Soman (GD), and also the "V" agents, principally VX. These are organophosphorus compounds chemically related to modern pesticides. The G agents, developed in the 1930s and 1940s, attack primarily through the respiratory system; the V agents, developed in the early 1950s, act by absorption through the skin. G agents can also attack through the skin if they have been mixed with a thickener that slows evaporation, keeping them in liquid form. All nerve agents injure and kill by binding to (and thus inhabiting the action of) acetylcholinesterase, an enzyme of the human body that is essential for the functioning of the nervous system; they produce a range of neurological disorders followed by paralysis, heart or respiratory failure, and death. Nerve agents are extremely toxic and usually kill very quickly — a drop the size of a pinhead can cause death within two to thirty minutes. Nerve agents are invisible, tasteless, and odorless. They cannot be detected without special equipment or until symptoms of exposure appear.

Chemical agents are distinguished from biological agents, which are living organisms, and from toxins, which are non-living chemical substances that are produced by living organisms (and now can be made through genetic engineering techniques).

Duration of Agent Potency

Chemical agents also are classified by the length of time they retain lethality on the battlefield. The simplest rule of thumb is

Mules and masked men drill for chemical war in November of 1918.

that a nonpersistent agent is effective for a matter of minutes after it is dispersed; a semipersistent agent for hours; and a persistent one for days.

For military employment, characteristics of persistence are of crucial importance. A persistent agent can slow an advancing enemy or hamper operations at a supply depot for days, but it usually makes no sense to deliver such a chemical in a way that will contaminate terrain that one's own forces plan to occupy. A nonpersistent agent, on the other hand, can be used effectively to force enemy troops to don protective gear; with proper timing and distance, the chemicals will have disappeared before friendly troops advance into the area.

Delivery Modes

Chemical agents can be delivered to targets by any usual munition—bombs, artillery and mortar shells, mines, rockets, and missiles—and, in addition, by spray tanks. The U.S. Department of Defense has proposed so-called binary munitions for its future chemical stockpile. Binary munitions use similar projectiles or containers to deliver the same chemical agents as ordinary (unitary) munitions. However, in binary munitions, relatively harmless components that can react to form lethal chemicals are kept separate and not mixed until the weapon is used; the chemical reaction that forms the lethal agent takes place after the munition is fired or launched.

Protection Against Chemical Agents

Because chemical agents attack by reacting chemically with the body, it is possible, if they can be kept away from the body, to provide protection against them. If a barrier that the agent cannot cross can be placed around the parts of the body that are vulnerable to the agent, the individual can remain unharmed. For some agents, this means a barrier around the respiratory system; for most modern agents it means one around the entire body.

The urgency of covering is greatest for nerve agents. The mask alone will protect against death from mustard agent; the burns are painful and temporarily disabling, but seldom fatal. Nerve agent absorbed through the skin, however, can result in death within a few minutes.

The United States, the Soviet Union, and U.S. European allies have developed individual protective gear well beyond the still-standard gas mask with an activated charcoal filter. In varying degrees they also have developed protective shelters, combat vehicles sealed against chemical agents, and procedures for decontaminating vehicles and equipment.

33

Although protection against chemical agents can be provided to some degree, to do so is not easy. And even if the protection works, it is enormously burdensome. It does not negate the military utility of chemicals or erase the advantage held by the side that initiates a chemical attack, especially if the targets are sufficiently transitory that the attackers themselves need not wear protective clothing. (And, of course, it does not protect civilians—who, if soldiers are protected, become the major chemical casualties in a chemical attack.) Infantry, computer operators, tank crews, aircraft ground crews, and pilots who must try to work in protective garments are far less effective than normal. Also, rapid detection of modern odorless and highly lethal agents is a particularly difficult aspect of defense. A central fact of modern chemical warfare is that defense to an increasingly uncertain degree is possible; but even effective defense is, at best, an enormous burden and military disadvantage.

Military Use

Chemical weapons used across a wide front tend to slow an attacking force, because of the need for cumbersome protective clothing. Targeting chemical attacks on specific and non-contiguous vulnerable points is more consistent with an offensive strategy.

Chemicals can also be used selectively to create weak spots in the line of defense. Military leaders emphasize that merely being able to force an enemy into defensive clothing because of expectation of a chemical attack, and thus to impede the functioning of encumbered personnel, creates an enormous military advantage, one that can extend up and down the front, far beyond the location of any actual use.

5   CHEMICAL WEAPONS: HISTORY AND OVERVIEW

CHEMICAL WARFARE IN THE 20TH CENTURY

Chemical Warfare Review Commission

An estimated 38 to 50 chemical agents were tried during the war, the most effective of which was mustard gas.

Although there are stories from antiquity and early modern history of noxious fumes being dispersed in battle, real chemical warfare begins with the First World War.

Chemicals in World War I

In the first months of the war, the French army released tear gas, a riot-control agent already used by police, and the Germans fired tear gas in artillery shells beginning in January 1915. The first use of lethal gas came in the ninth month of the war on April 22, 1915, near Ypres, Belgium. In a carefully prepared attack, German soldiers opened the valves on more than 5,000 cylinders of chlorine, sending a miles-long cloud of gas toward the French trenches. Two French divisions, one an elite unit, panicked and fled, opening a five-mile gap in the Allied lines. However, the German commanders, who had been skeptical of the new weapon, had not assembled enough reserves to exploit the breakthrough. During the night the Allies pushed up reinforcements to close the gap, and never again did gas have such dramatic tactical success.

This reading was excerpted fro the June 1985 "Report of the Chemical Warfare Review Commission." The Commission was established by Congress and its presidentially appointed members included former National Security Affairs Assistant Zbigniew Brzezinski and retired Army General Alexander Haig, Jr.

Within a few days Allied troops were using makeshift protective respirators — squares of women's hat veiling stuffed with cotton waste and impregnated with photographer's "hypo" solution, or handkerchiefs wet with urine, tied over the nose and mouth. There were more instances of panic during gas attacks, but none on a large scale, and on several occasions troops moved forward through gas clouds to reinforce the front lines.

Within a few months the Allies had their own lethal gas, and by the end of 1916 all the warring powers had chemical weapons, as well as gas masks to provide reasonably effective protection against them. The protection, however, did not mean that chemicals thereafter were considered useless. Poison gas attacks steadily increased throughout the war. In fact, most of the World War I chemical munitions were expended in the last year, 1918. Chemicals seem to have been regarded by troops and commanders as little different in moral terms from other weapons. In the postwar period, however, they came to symbolize the horrors of modern war and were looked upon with disdain by many military officers as well as civilians.

Throughout World War I, there was a constant effort to develop new agents and new tactics that would overcome the enemy's countermeasures. An estimated 38 to 50 chemical agents were tried during the war, the most effective of which was mustard gas, which the Germans developed methods to produce in quantity and began using in 1917. Although its persistence made it useless for pre-attack preparation fires, it was a formidable delayer of enemy advances. The Germans also used mustard agent to neutralize artillery batteries and supply operations, and for preventing defending Allied troops from bringing up reserves. Because it penetrated boots and uniforms to cause painful burns, gas masks alone could not fully protect against it.

Gas tactics stressed surprise, to catch enemy troops without masks. Efforts were also made to induce unmasking. Sometimes, for example, a relatively nonlethal agent that could penetrate the mask and cause coughing or vomiting would be used to force unmasking at the same time that a lethal agent was fired. Delivery means, besides the original pressure cylinders, included artillery shells, mortars, and "projectors" that lobbed canisters of agent into enemy trenches.

In all, World War I saw approximately 1.3 million gas casualties, of which about 92,000 (7 percent) were fatal.

French soldiers with M-2 masks advance through a gas cloud.

Source: United States Department of Defense

Chemical weapons in World War I were not a decisive weapon, but were effective for a number of specific military purposes, and were used more and more as the war lengthened, even though during its last months the war became more mobile. By the end the Germans, according to one source, were using high-explosive shells and chemical shells in a ratio of 50:50.

The Washington Treaty of 1922 outlawed the use in war (except in retaliation) of lethal poisonous gases and similar substances. It was ratified by the United States but never went into force because France, one of the five signatory powers, failed to ratify it. Three years later, the Geneva Protocol, containing language identical to that of the Washington Treaty, and drafted by the U.S. delegation, was signed by the United States and 28 other countries, including the Soviet Union. However, it was not ratified by the U.S. Senate. The United States continued to abide by the 1925 Geneva Protocol, and finally ratified it in 1975.

Nonuse in World War II

When World War II began in 1939, most of the belligerents were opposed to the use of chemical weapons and were not fully prepared to use them. Great Britain, for example, did not begin to acquire a retaliatory capability until less than a year before the war started. Italy had used mustard gas against

37

Ethiopian troops in 1935 and 1936, in violation of the Geneva Protocol and to the outrage of leaders and the public in most countries. But although the warring powers had only small amounts of chemical munitions at the beginning of the war, these increased so sharply that by 1945 the total stockpile far exceeded the total chemical munitions used in World War I. Qualitatively the agents were more deadly also, because nerve agents had been discovered and developed, first in Germany and then elsewhere, in the 1930s. Germany made the first nerve agent (GA) in 1936, built the first pilot plant in 1939, and had manufactured 12,000 tons by 1945.

Beginning in the 1930s and continuing as late as 1944, Japan, which was much better armed chemically than China and did not fear retaliation, used some chemical agents against Chinese armies and civilians. However, it never used chemicals against the United States, and none of the other belligerent powers used chemicals militarily during the war. During the first years, 1939-43, the powers appear to have been largely self-deterred—by their commitment to a no-first-use policy, or by the judgment that chemical use would not be tactically advantageous.

During 1943-45, fear of strategic chemical retaliation seems to have deterred use of chemicals at several points where combatants were tempted to use them. The British and German leaders saw their cities as hostages to chemical attack. In May

1942, Prime Minister Churchill had committed Britain to retaliation against German cities if Germany used chemicals against the Soviet Union. The following month, President Franklin D. Roosevelt (who in 1920 had served on an advisory committee to the Washington Disarmament Conference that led to the 1922 treaty, and personally loathed chemical warfare) threatened retaliation against Japan if it did not cease using toxic weapons against the Chinese. In 1943 he warned that the United States would reply to enemy use of chemicals with "full and swift retaliation in kind." By that time the Allies were gaining overwhelming air superiority. The British, at the same time, despite air superiority, were restrained by the German buzz-bombs and V-2 rockets, which they knew could be armed with chemicals.

In the last months of the war in the Pacific, there was little militarily to deter U.S. use of chemicals against the Japanese, and there loomed the prospect of an estimated 1,000,000 Allied casualties—nearly all Americans—from an invasion of the Japanese home islands. Army Chief of Staff General George C. Marshall was persuaded that gas would be useful in mopping-up operations that otherwise would take great numbers of American lives. Admiral William D. Leahy, however, Roosevelt's senior military advisor and *de facto* Chairman of the Joint Chiefs of Staff, resisted, citing President Roosevelt's unequivocal renunciation of first-use. With the dropping of atomic bombs on Hiroshima and Nagasaki, the war against Japan ended without the issue of chemicals being revisited.

Since World War II

There have been several instances of use of lethal chemical agents in war in the past twenty-five years. The frequency appears to have been increasing, and during the past five years the world has seen the first instance of lethal chemical use in war by a major power—the Soviet Union—since World War I. Lethal chemical weapons have been used:

- By the Egyptians in Yemen, 1963-67.
- By the Vietnamese in Laos and Cambodia in the late 1970s, including biological toxins, perhaps supplied by the Soviet Union.
- By the Soviet Union in Afghanistan, beginning in the early 1980s. Intelligence information made available to the Commission supports the conclusion that not only

well-known lethal chemical agents, but also new, experimental agents, and also biological toxins, have been used by the Soviets in Afghanistan repeatedly and systematically.

- In the Iran-Iraq war, by Iraq. A United Nations investigating panel of scientists from neutral countries reported that mustard agent clearly has been used. Recent reports are that in addition Iraq may have used nerve gas and perhaps also new lethal substances.

In the future, other countries are likely to use chemical agents because not only are they effective but they are also relatively inexpensive and easy to acquire.

6   CHEMICAL WEAPONS: HISTORY AND OVERVIEW

IRAQ'S CHEMICAL WAR AGAINST THE KURDS

Robert Mullen Cook-Deegan, M.D.

We defined a "severe" profile of injury to include symptoms of eye irritation; shortness of breath or pain on breathing; skin blistering; and vomiting.

We entered two refugee camps in southeastern Turkey, one containing 5,100 and the other 13,100 people who had fled northern Iraq. There we elicited consistent accounts of poison gas attacks, from bombs dropped by aircraft, releasing a foul-smelling, yellow-gray cloud. Small animal and fowl died within minutes, and people near the bomb bursts began to die soon after. Their skin turned black, and blood-tinged fluid oozed from their noses and mouths. Their skin became thick and leathery after death. Eyewitnesses did not describe shrapnel wounds.

The attacks were against both civilian villages and Pesh Merga (Kurdish fighter) encampments. Eighteen of those completing our survey (69 percent) were civilians; 8 were Pesh Merga soldiers (31 percent). Their ages ranged from 6 to 70.

Robert Cook-Deegan was one of three doctors representing the Physicians for Human Rights that went to Turkey in 1988 to investigate alleged Iraqi poison gas attacks against its own minority Kurdish population. This reading was excerpted from Dr. Cook-Deegan's testimony before the Senate Committee on Governmental Affairs, February 9, 1989.

Refugees Describe Symptoms

Those who survived described a complex of symptoms: difficulty breathing; burning throat; eyes burning and watering; runny nose; dizziness; nausea; vomiting; and headache. Their skin itched, oozing a clear yellowish fluid, and then formed large blisters filled with clear amber-colored fluid. Each of these symptoms was reported by over 65 percent of the 27 people who completed a 120-item questionnaire designed for this mission. We defined a "severe" profile of injury to include symptoms of eye irritation; shortness of breath or pain on breathing; skin blistering; and vomiting. Just under half of those within 250 meters of bomb bursts (8 of 17) had all four symptoms. These are the symptoms one would expect of poison gas.

One 70-year-old woman described the attack to us this way: "All of a sudden my eyes became blurry . . . and I became short of breath and felt terribly weak. It had a bad smell like garlic and my mouth became bitter. About two minutes later, I began to feel sick and after that my skin felt like it was burning. I saw a lot of animals die before I felt sick—birds, chickens, hens, cattle, sheep, goats. And then I had difficulty breathing, my skin was burning, my eyes were burning and my nose was running. There was water oozing from my skin, my face and hands. The fluid was coming out yellowish, coming out from my skin which was severely burning and itching too."

We were able to compare answers of those attacked in the same villages but, at the time of our visit, living in different Turkish refugee camps. The camps were separated by over 100 kilometers, so these refugees had not been able to communicate. This gave us a good cross-check on details of the attack, and enabled us to verify that their accounts were indeed consistent. Those closer to bomb bursts were also more likely to have severe symptoms, as one would expect. We concluded that lethal poison gas was used against the Kurds on August 25, 1988. (Other Kurds from different parts of Iraq described attacks on other dates, but these were not included in our survey.)

Several weeks after we returned to the United States, we learned of another investigative team's findings. Gwynne Roberts, a freelance journalist for British television, had entered northern Iraq and taken soil samples from areas allegedly attacked. Analysis showed degradation products of sulfur mustard (yperite), a blistering poison gas that the German military began to use in World War I.

Our findings are consistent with the use of mustard gas, but mustard gas may not explain all our findings. The reports of death beginning within five minutes indicate that probably additional agents were employed, but several lethal chemicals are consistent with this finding of sudden death, and we cannot say definitively which were used. This should not obscure the more important conclusion, concurred with by several chemical weapons specialists, that the government of Iraq had used lethal poison gas against its own citizens.

Eyewitness Account

My description of the events is perhaps somewhat technical. I think the true meaning of our findings is better expressed in the words of an eight-year-old girl whom we met in the Mardin refugee camp. Aagiza lived in the village of Ekmala, and had not spoken at all for five weeks after the attacks, until a few days before we visited with her. At the time of the attack, she was several hundred meters away from her home tending livestock. One bomb hit near her house, where her mother, father, and 20-year-old brother were: "I saw two airplanes overhead and they dropped some bomb, it made smoke, yellowish-white smoke. It had a bad smell like DDT, the powder they kill insects with. It had a bitter taste. After I smelled the gas, my nose began to run and my eyes became blurry and I could not see and my eyes started watering too. And I still have some of the effects like my blurry vision and I have these things (skin blisters) over my chest. I saw my parents fall down with my brother after the attack, and they told me they were dead. I looked at their skin and it was black and they weren't moving. And I was scared and crying and I did not know what to do. I saw their skin turn dark and blood was coming out from their mouths and from their noses. I wanted to touch them, but they stopped me and I started crying again."

After these events, Aagiza left with her sisters, her younger brother, and her grandmother. They traveled several days over arduous mountain passes into Turkey, where they had been living for over a month at the time of our visit. When we interviewed her, Aagiza had no idea where she would be living in two months or even two weeks.

A Dual Catastrophe

Our survey documents one small fragment of a dual catastrophe. The Iraqi chemical weapons attack on the Kurds is a catastrophe, first of all, in terms of the deaths, the injuries and the human suffering we have described. We may never know the true total of casualties; what we already know, however, fully justifies the conclusion that this was a premeditated public health disaster.

But this is a catastrophe in a second and even larger sense. It represents a major and dangerous breach in the international agreement that human beings, no matter what the circumstances of war, rebellion, or conflict, should never be subjected to poison gas or other chemical weapons. It is not merely human beings who are assaulted in such an attack; it is our common humanity. As physicians, we call for a total ban on the development, manufacture, deployment and use of these agents.

CONFLICTING SOCIAL VALUES

This activity may be used as an individualized study guide for students in libraries and resource centers or as a discussion catalyst in small group and classroom discussions.

Are chemical weapons less moral than standard conventional weapons? This question of conflicting social values has been around for a long time. Even before the mass use of poison gas in World War I, the question confronted officers of the British High Command in 1854. During their war with the Russian Czar Nicholas, the British pondered the use of sulphur gas against the Russian garrison at Sebastpol. Ultimately it was decided that the use of sulphur gas was against all the rules of "civilized warfare". They then proceeded to employ a new high velocity rifle, the "bouquet" (a number of small grenades encased in a larger one), and the new shell known as "Whistling Dick" which blew off heads and shredded internal organs most efficiently.

Today the world condemns Iraq's use of chemical agents including mustard gas (which blisters body tissue), and nerve agents that can cause respiratory failure in minutes. To counter the Iraqi threat, the U.S. employed such "civilized weapons" as napalm (which adheres to the skin and burns) and cluster bombs (the modern version of the Crimean "bouquet").

Is poison gas less moral than napalm? Who must decide this question of conflicting social values? Should all weapons be abolished or should we look upon all weapons as did Prince Andrei in *War and Peace* who said "the object of warfare is murder."

GUIDELINES

Questions of social conflict are often very complex and include political, religious, ethnic/racial, cultural and personal considerations. After reading the statement above, respond to the following:

1. Explain why someone might believe chemical weapons to be immoral on political, religious or cultural grounds.

2. On what basis might one argue that chemical weapons are no less moral than many "conventional" weapons.

3. What is the prevailing attitude of the international leadership? Of the world's religions? Of the medical profession?

4. What criteria must be used to determine the difference between "moral" and "immoral" weapons? Be specific.

5. If the character of Prince Andrei in the novel *War and Peace* is indeed correct, then how should the international community deal with the proliferation and use of chemical weapons?

6. Consider how you stand personally. Which of the considerations listed above would you base your own opinion on?

CHAPTER 3

U.S. CHEMICAL WARFARE PROGRAM IN VIETNAM: POINTS AND COUNTERPOINTS

CHEMICAL WARFARE: THE POINT

OPERATION RANCH HAND: THE MILITARY PERSPECTIVE

William A. Buckingham, Jr.

William Buckingham is a historian at the U.S. Government's Office of Air Force History in Washington D.C. The following reading highlights his research on the U.S. Air Force use of herbicides during the Vietnam War and the military's justification for its policy, code named "Operation Ranch Hand."

Points to Consider:

1. What was the scope of herbicide use in South Vietnam during the nine years of Operation Ranch Hand?

2. Cite examples from the reading where the military concluded that the programs were successful and should be continued. Why were the programs considered successful?

3. What did the National Academy of Sciences (NAS) study conclude about the effects of pesticide use on humans and the ecology?

Excerpted from a book by William A. Buckingham, Jr., entitled **Operation Ranch Hand: The Air Force and Herbicides in Southeast Asia, 1961-1971,** Office of Air Force History, U.S.A.F., 1982.

In sum, the team found that the technical and military effectiveness of defoliation and crop destruction was high.

In 1961, President Ngo Dinh Diem of South Vietnam asked the United States to conduct aerial herbicide spraying in his country. In August of that year, the South Vietnamese Air Force initiated herbicide operations with American help.

Operation Ranch Hand, the designation for the program, began in January 1962. Gradually limitations were relaxed and the spraying became more frequent, and covered larger areas. By the time it ended nine years later, some eighteen million gallons of chemicals had been sprayed on an estimated twenty percent of South Vietnam's jungles, including thirty-six percent of its mangrove forests. The Air Force also carried out herbicide operations in Laos from December 1965 to September 1969 with the permission of the Laotian government.

Early Proposals

The Combat Development and Test Center (CDTC) developed a massive operational program on the basis of favorable results from tests on manioc and on jungle foliage. The plan had four goals:

a. Stripping the Cambodian-Laotian-North Vietnam border of foliage to remove protective cover from Viet Cong reinforcements;

b. Defoliating a portion of the Mekong Delta area known as "Zone D" in which the Viet Cong had numerous bases;

c. Destroying numerous abandoned manioc groves which the Viet Cong used as food sources;

d. Destroying mangrove swamps within which the Viet Cong took refuge.

This proposal envisioned the defoliation of 31,250 square miles of jungle, an area equivalent to about half of South Vietnam! In addition, the proposal called for spraying 1,125 square miles of mangrove swamps and 312.5 square miles of manioc.

Another suggested defoliation program of lesser scope devised by American officials in Saigon replaced the massive CDTC program. This more limited plan consisted of three sequential programs. Phase I, to begin within twenty days,

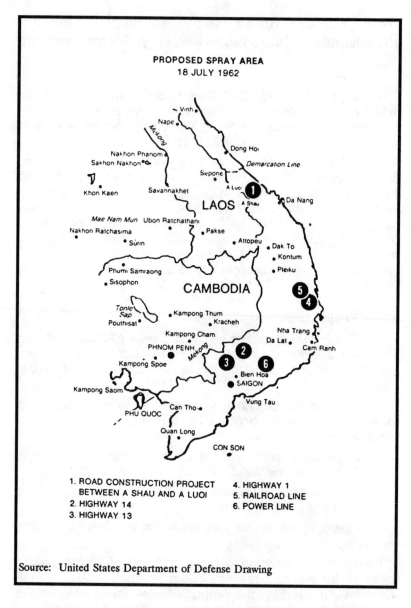

PROPOSED SPRAY AREA
18 JULY 1962

1. ROAD CONSTRUCTION PROJECT
   BETWEEN A SHAU AND A LUOI
2. HIGHWAY 14
3. HIGHWAY 13
4. HIGHWAY 1
5. RAILROAD LINE
6. POWER LINE

Source: United States Department of Defense Drawing

would spray 334.5 square miles of manioc and rice crops with 2,4,5-T and cacodylic acid. The second phase would begin within 65 days, last about thirty days and defoliate 200 square miles of jungle in Zone D with 2,4-D and 2,4,5-T. This second phase would be coordinated with military actions. During Phase

III, certain unspecified border areas would be selectively defoliated.

Crop Destruction Begins

Chemically destroying Viet Cong crops had been considered since planning for the use of herbicides in South Vietnam began in 1961. The South Vietnamese, already destroying what they considered to be Viet Cong crops by pulling, cutting, burning, strafing and dropping napalm, held chemical herbicides to be merely a cheaper and more efficient way of fighting the war.

On October 2, 1962, President Kennedy decided to allow restricted crop destruction to proceed.

As the Joint Chiefs and others had recommended, Secretary McNamara discussed crop destruction at his Hawaii conference on October 8. He directed that the first targets be sprayed as quickly as possible and that the effectiveness of these operations be rapidly evaluated.

The base for this first crop destruction operation was the airstrip at Nui Ba Ra in Phuoc Long Province. On the night of November 20, a solution of "blue" herbicide (cacodylic acid) was prepared, and 200 gallons of this water-based mixture filled the tanks of five helicopters. In total, the helicopters sprayed about 700 gallons of "blue", or 300 gallons less than planned, on about 400 acres of crops.

Both American and Vietnamese evaluators rated the results of this first crop destruction operation as generally successful. Within five hours of the first spray runs, a U.S. observer on the ground noticed that plants were wilted and discolored around the edges. Less than ten hours after spraying, another group of

Americans saw that bean, peanut, potato, and manioc plants had all turned black. Two days later aerial observation by General Harkins and others found that all the sprayed crops, including rice, were brown. Photo reconnaissance missions five and seven days after the spraying showed that the brown color had deepened and that the crops were completely destroyed. A report on the operation prepared by a team headed by General Delmore estimated that the herbicide had destroyed 745,000 pounds of food, enough to feed 1,000 Viet Cong for more than a year.

Effectiveness of Defoliation

Ranch Hand got back into the spray business in June 1963, when the unit began applying herbicides along 46 kilometers of canals on the Ca Mau peninsula. Eight sorties, dispensing 7,200 gallons of chemicals, were flown in this region of IV Corps between June 6 and 9.

A message from the Secretary of State required that a full report and evaluation of all 1963 herbicide operations to date be sent to Washington. On September 4, 1963, a team was appointed to conduct this evaluation and prepare a report. U.S. Army Lt. Col. Peter G. Olenchuk headed the team.

The Olenchuk Report rated the military worth of defoliation and crop destruction as high. The team found that improved visibility had eased the problem of providing security in defoliated areas, had made aerial surveillance much more effective, and had enabled ground security forces to be reduced. Defoliation had also created an increased field of fire for troops on the ground, a benefit which, however, accrued to both South Vietnamese troops and the Viet Cong. In view of the reluctance of the Viet Cong to operate in defoliated areas, the evaluation team concluded that the South Vietnamese derived the most benefit from this effect. In sum, the team found that the technical and military effectiveness of defoliation and crop destruction was high.

On April 30, 1965, Ranch Hand began the largest defoliation project attempted to that time, "Operation Swamp Fox." Swamp Fox covered designated coastal areas of Bac Lieu, Vinh Binh, and Ba Xuyen provinces in the Mekong Delta. Much of the Viet Cong activity in the Delta depended on strongholds, generally immune from attack, where they had training camps, arms factories, repair facilities, and hospitals. Shallow draft sampans could easily bring in supplies and escape aerial detection beneath the foliage of the dense mangrove swamps which covered the area, foliage which herbicides could remove. Defoliation missions against this area flown by Ranch Hand began on April 30, 1965, and continued through May 25. Ranch Hand received orders from 2nd Air Division to halt flights over the Delta target complex after spraying only 70 percent of the planned area because of the heavy ground fire encountered.

During 1965, crop destruction acreage constituted 42 percent of the total land area covered by herbicides, with the remainder sprayed for defoliation. Although the 65,949 acres of crops sprayed in 1965 was less than a third of the crop area sprayed in the peak year of 1967, the ratio of crop destruction acreage to defoliation acreage peaked in 1965. Washington significantly relaxed controls on crop destruction during the year, making the approval for such operations much easier to obtain.

Operations Expand into Laos

In December 1965, the Ranch Hand area of operations was expanded to include parts of southern and eastern Laos traversed by the Ho Chi Minh Trail—a complex of roads and foot paths used by the North Vietnamese to infiltrate men and supplies into South Vietnam. The North Vietnamese had significantly increased their use of these routes during the year, as U.S. forces and ground combat activity increased in South Vietnam. Accordingly, stopping or slowing this infiltration through Laos became a major concern.

By June 30, 1966, Ranch Hand had sprayed approximately 1,500 kilometers of roads and trails to a depth of 250 meters on each side—the result of 200 sorties and about 200,000 gallons of herbicides. Fighter pilots and forward air controllers, who often recommended targets, credited the defoliation effort with a major role in the destruction of more than 1,000 trucks which were caught on these roads.

At about the same time that defoliation missions began in Laos, General Westmoreland received authorization to conduct crop destruction operations in that country. Ranch Hand destroyed some crops in Laos, but such missions never became a major part of the herbicide program.

The Peak Years: 1966-67

At the same time Ranch Hand was flying missions in Laos in early 1966, other spray activity was taking place in South

Vietnam. During January, UC-123s flew 130 sorties and delivered 118,500 gallons of herbicide against targets in the Pleiky, Vung Tau, Bac Lieu, Saigon, and Nha Trang areas. Half that amount was used on Laotian targets.

In 1966 Ranch Hand received permission to spray an area that, though small geographically, was very important militarily—the southern portion of the Demilitarized Zone separating North Vietnam from South Vietnam. Infiltration by North Vietnamese troops across the DMZ was a significant threat to U.S. and South Vietnamese troops in the I Corps. Defoliation there would help to uncover infiltration routes and supply stockpiles.

The main areas of Ranch Hand activity during January, February, and March 1967, however, were War Zones C and D, with sortie levels as high as 29 per day.

This period also saw the third and last large-scale intentional effort combining defoliation with incendiaries to produce a forest fire in South Vietnam. Codenamed "Pink Rose," the operation involved three target areas, one in War Zone D and two in War Zone C. Each target consisted of a square, seven kilometers on each side, encompassing about 12,000 acres of heavily canopied jungle.

The three areas, designated A, B, and C, had received their initial treatment of herbicide by November 27, 1966. Ranch Hand covered areas A and B with "orange", while spraying area C with "white", a new mixture introduced to help alleviate the shortage of orange. The first coverage was at the normal rate of three gallons per acre. It was followed by a second dose of the same herbicides in January 1967. Aerial reconnaissance of the targets found that the herbicide effects were equal to or better than what had been expected, and inspection teams found good drying throughout. Ranch Hand flew over two hundred UC-123 sorties and sprayed 255,000 gallons of herbicide in accomplishing its part in Pink Rose.

In July, Ranch Hand lost its fourth aircraft downed during a spray mission. The entire crew, three officers and one enlisted man, perished. July was, however, a big month for herbicide delivery, with 435,805 gallons dispensed in 536 spray sorties. Activity increased toward the end of the year, with an average of over 500,000 gallons of herbicides delivered each month during October, November, and December.

Side Effects

Even as the sorties decreased, ecological problems continued to surface. Unintended damage from storage drums and accidental leakage was remedied, but emergency dumps remained a problem. In the early part of 1969, residents of Da Nang noticed that large numbers of shade trees were dead or dying and that garden plots had also suffered damage, probably from herbicides. Investigation eliminated spray drift as a cause, and suspicion centered on "empty" herbicide drums which individuals had moved and stored throughout the city. Unfortunately, when the herbicide was drained from these drums, as much as two or three gallons remained inside. The combination of herbicide orange's oily base and the small openings in the drums made it difficult to remove the residue. Vaporization of the herbicide as people moved and stored the drums had caused the damage to vegetation. The local people had also employed the drums as containers for water, diesel fuel, and gasoline. The burning of herbicide-contaminated fuel in motorcycles and other vehicles added to the problem.

The NAS Study

The U.S. Congress finally mandated in a law signed by President Nixon on October 7, 1970, the extensive study, demanded by scientists, of the effects of herbicides in South Vietnam. Congress further directed the Secretary of Defense to contract with the National Academy of Sciences (NAS) for this investigation.

The NAS investigators failed to find any clear evidence of direct damage to human health from herbicides. However, they did discover a consistent pattern of largely second-hand reports from Montagnards claiming that occasionally herbicides had caused acute or fatal respiratory problems in children. On the controversial question of herbicide-related human birth defects, the NAS could likewise find no evidence substantiating a link in spite of making a considerable effort. The President of the NAS concluded:

On balance, the effects of the herbicide program on the health of South Vietnamese people appear to have been smaller than one might have feared.

As was the case with humans, NAS found that the effects of the herbicide spraying program on land and vegetation were also less than some scientists had suspected. The main impact of herbicides on vegetation was the immediate killing effect resulting from direct contact with the spray. Since the herbicides disappeared quickly in the soil, they had no significant effects on plants during the next growing season.

CHEMICAL WARFARE: THE COUNTERPOINT

CHEMICAL ECOCIDE IN VIETNAM CONTINUES

Peter Korn

Peter Korn is a free-lance reporter based in Portland, Oregon. The reading that follows is a highlighted version of his article on the terrible legacy of pesticide use in Southeast Asia during the Vietnam War, which appeared in the Amicus *Journal.*

Points to Consider:

1. How were the soil and landscape affected by U.S. chemical warfare in Vietnam? How has wildlife been affected?

2. Describe some of the medical problems being experienced by Vietnamese civilians and U.S. veterans exposed to Agent Orange.

3. How are dioxins suspected in the idea of gene pool manipulation?

4. How would U.S. recognition of and assistance to Vietnam ease the burden on hospitals in Vietnam?

Excerpted from an article by Peter Korn titled "Vietnam Continues," **The Amicus Journal,** Winter, 1990, pp. 10-16.

About 10 percent of the total area of South Vietnam was sprayed with 20 million gallons of herbicides. According to Vietnamese scientists, 12 percent of inland forests and 40 percent of the coastal mangrove forests were sprayed at least once.

In a village near the Kampuchean border, a Vietnamese farmer quits work for the day. His field is just beginning to take shape, but the task seems insurmountable, as if he is working against the will of the earth he seeks to till. Around him, barren hard-baked, cracked dirt stretches for miles. An occasional skeleton of a tree dots the landscape, bare finger-like limbs pointing down, appropriately forlorn sentinels surveying the sorry scene. The land surrounding the farm is pockmarked with nearly symmetrical holes — bomb craters — empty now as they await the summer rains. Distant green hills circle the field, part of the jungle that stretches farther than the farmer has ever traveled. This spot was once a jungle, too, before the war.

A few miles away, in the village of Tan Lap, a woman gives birth at the small hospital that serves the area. The doctor wonders, "How will this one look? Will it greet the world complete?" Too many times he has observed infants born with missing limbs and other major defects. Not so many now, only two or three a year. The horrors seem to be abating. But many of the adults in the area have begun to develop liver ailments, including cancer, the doctor has noticed.

Chemical Victims

These people and their land are victims of the most modern war instruments — chemicals — specifically, Agent Orange. They are also the victims of tragic American neglect.

The last American soldier left Vietnam nearly fifteen years ago. The last drum of Agent Orange, the dioxin-laced herbicide used to defoliate South Vietnam, was sprayed in 1971. America still does not recognize Vietnam. Our government enforces a trade embargo with that country. It is as if by pretending diplomatically that Vietnam does not exist, we can collectively disown any responsibility for our actions there.

From 1961 to 1971, the United States resorted to a massive defoliation program in fighting the Vietnam War. North Vietnamese soldiers had infiltrated the South using dense forests

and jungle, often in areas adjacent to American bases, as cover. The defoliation campaign was designed to destroy the forests and jungle, eliminating the cover. From a military standpoint, the campaign was eminently successful.

About 10 percent of the total area of South Vietnam was sprayed with 20 million gallons of herbicides. According to Vietnamese scientists, 12 percent of inland forests and 40 percent of the coastal mangrove forests were sprayed at least once. Many areas received repeated sprayings, and farmers and their families were often doused in the chemicals. As these toxins lingered in the soil and the food chain, the Vietnamese lived in constant exposure to them.

Agent Orange is the best known of the defoliating compounds, and was the most widely used. Twelve million gallons of the mixture of the herbicides 2,4-D and 2,4,5-T, containing the dioxin 2,3,7,8-TCDD, were sprayed in Vietnam, mostly on forested areas. In experiments with laboratory animals, dioxin has been shown to cause birth defects as a teratogen, genetic damage as a mutagen, and cancer as a carcinogen. Less known agents White, a mixture of 2,4-D and picloran, and Blue, a form of cacodylic acid containing arsenic, were also used, the latter for the destruction of agricultural crops.

Changes in the Soil

In addition to destroying trees and brush, in time these herbicides changed the composition of the soil, killing microorganisms, turning once fecund land infertile, and interrupting the natural cycle of succeeding species. Some devastated forests have remained lifeless, while others became savannahs, dominated by hardy grasses and bamboo.

Observing the changes in their landscape, rural Vietnamese developed a sort of botanical mythology. As planes and helicopters moved over the landscape dropping their payloads, peasants watched the forests disappear and an unfamiliar coarse grass take root. This grass would often catch fire, completing the design of eliminating cover for North Vietnamese troops, and making the land barren. The Vietnamese believed the Americans were dropping grass seed along with the defoliants and began calling the plant American Grass. Large areas of American Grass, actually *Imperata cylindrica,* still thrive in South Vietnam. Scientists know it to be a species native to southeast Asia, but once forest and jungle have taken hold, it is rarely able to compete. Defoliants cleared the way for the Imperata to take over.

Devastated Landscape

Many of the defoliated trees remain, now standing dead

snags. During the dry season, they provide kindling for fires which continue the cycle of destruction. Hillsides have eroded, washing topsoil out to sea. Without water-retaining vegetation, floods have increased during the rainy season and droughts in the dry season. In some areas, the dioxin persisted in the soil and nothing was able to grow up to ten years after the spraying.

The country's natural dry season impedes regeneration of forests, so it soon became obvious to the Vietnamese that replanting was necessary if the forests were to return. But the Vietnamese also contributed to the problem. In the Ma Da forest, grasses and young trees did take root after the spraying, but settlers in need of more land for agriculture burned off the new growth to begin farming. In time, most of the herbicides washed off hilly areas and into the lowlands, then into the food chain, and eventually into population centers.

The Vietnamese government has allocated little money for research into the dioxin's effect on natural resources. Only a few isolated tests have been made to determine its persistence in soil. Ten samples of silt from Vietnamese rivers have been analyzed in the last twenty years, hardly enough on which to base any findings.

Effect on Wildlife

Wildlife was also affected by the spraying, as habitats were destroyed and altered. Villagers claim that in the days after heavy spraying wild and domestic birds and mammals died, whether from the toxic effects of herbicides or indirectly, from starvation, is unknown. One Vietnamese study compared the A Luoi Valley, which had been sprayed, with two unsprayed control forests. In the unsprayed forests there were 145 and 170 bird species respectively. In A Luoi there were only 24 species of birds. There were 30 and 55 mammal species in the control forests, respectively. In A Luoi, there were only five. Vietnamese scientists asked about dioxin levels in wildlife say they do not have the funds for laboratory tests on wildlife – only one turtle and one snake have been tested; both retained high levels of dioxin.

The Human Toll

And yet, the ecological disaster of Vietnam can be seen most vividly in the country's hospitals. What little funding the government has been able to put together has gone mostly to study the diseases and congenital malformations dioxin appears to be causing among its citizens. The results of these studies, unfamiliar to most Western physicians and scientists, hint at, rather than tells a story.

To understand why so little data on the effects of dioxin has been produced by the Vietnamese, it is necessary to visit a Vietnamese hospital. And when the subject is the teratogenic effects of dioxin, the hospital to visit is Tu Du Maternity Hospital in Ho Chi Minh City, formerly Saigon.

On the second floor of Tu Du there is a room identified by a sign above the door as Trung Bay, "Exhibition Room." Wooden shelves line the walls of the room, five-gallon glass jars fill the shelves. Each jar holds a lifeless fetus, some stillborn, others aborted. The fetuses are horribly deformed. Some lack limbs; others, victims of anencephaly, are missing brains. Each is a clue to the mystery of dioxin, a possible result of a mother's exposure to Agent Orange.

In the midst of this macabre scene stands Nguyen Thi Ngoc Phuong, Tu Du Hospital's deputy director. Phuong is something of a folk hero in Vietnam. She is written about in newspapers, and a movie has even been made about her life. She is the lifeblood of this woeful hospital.

Medical System Can't Keep Up

Medical supplies are low in Vietnam. Tu Du's doctors and midwives make do with blunt scissors when severing umbilical cords and reuse supposedly sterile surgical gloves up to ten times. The equipment is ancient. Thirty-year-old incubators lack oxygen regulation, and the hospital's only fetal heart monitor is broken. The hospital has run out of painkillers, even aspirin. Virtually nothing has come from America since the end of the war.

For fifteen years, Phuong has confronted the effects of Agent Orange as she has delivered child after child with birth defects. She can point out examples of each of these defects in the jars of her exhibition room, and in some cases, in the patients around her.

Vietnam's medical system is barely able to keep up with the country's ill. There are few funds left over for research. The country is one of the poorest in the world and can afford only about $10,000 a year for dioxin research.

With little money and less time, Phuong and her Vietnamese

colleagues have done what they can, acting as epidemiologists, and sometimes accepting the assistance of the few Western physicians who have made their way here. She knows the studies contain epidemiological flaws. But their combined weight represents a substantial foundation toward an indictment of Agent Orange.

In one study, Phuong and a colleague compared two South Vietnamese communities: heavily-sprayed Thanh Phong and an unsprayed district of Ho Chi Minh City. Physicians and nurses interviewed mothers and offspring to determine exposure to herbicides and medical histories. All of the 1,249 women from Thanh Phong were determined to have been directly exposed.

Phuong's study showed women in the exposed village were more likely to undergo spontaneous abortions (up to twelve weeks). The odds of fetal death in utero (twenty weeks or more) were 26.6 times greater in Thanh Phuong. The odds of congenital abnormalities in the women from Thanh Phuong were 2.5 times greater than in the women in Ho Chi Minh City. Since Vietnamese researchers lack training to identify the hidden abnormalities which actually comprise the majority of birth defects, studies can focus only on externally detectable defects.

The Vietnamese have conducted other studies, but they are far from definitive by Western public health standards. One study compared the outcomes of pregnancies among wives of North Vietnamese soldiers. One group of soldiers had fought in the South and had been exposed to herbicides, the other group had not. None of the wives were exposed. This study showed a 38 percent increase in major birth defects and a 19 percent increase in spontaneous abortions after paternal exposure to herbicides.

One horrible hypothesis raised by Vietnamese scientists is that the dioxin has actually mutated the chromosomes of the exposed men. Western scientists downplay this possibility, but if it is true, the genetic pool, and thus the health of future Vietnamese generations, have all been altered by the Vietnam War.

Vietnamese physicians connect a number of other health problems to the dioxin in the blood of their citizens. Liver cancer, soft tissue cancer, lymphoma, and lung cancer have all been cited in studies. Rates of diseases such as malaria and dengue fever have increased in sprayed areas, posing the possibility that dioxin is responsible for a wide range of maladies through its effects on the immune system.

More Dioxin Research Needed

Dr. Arnold Schechter, professor of preventive medicine at the State University of New York at Binghamton has been studying dioxins for more than a decade. He cites municipal incinerators, paper and pulp mills, and even store-bought milk as sources of dioxin in the United States.

Schechter has sought funding to pursue research in Vietnam that might lead to conclusive knowledge about the effects of dioxin, but he has met with great resistance. The National Institutes of Health (NIH) and Environmental Protection Agency (EPA) have yielded nothing, he says, citing politics as the reason. Large foundations seem wary of becoming connected to anything involving Vietnam or Agent Orange.

The lack of medical assistance from the United States to Vietnam appalls Schechter as much as the lack of research interest. "We can do with peaceful methods what we were unsuccessful doing with the war," he says.

Lucien Adanhaim, a French epidemiologist, has been trying for three years to secure funding for a broad-based study of health in Vietnam that would entail collecting hundreds of tissue samples to be brought back to Western laboratories for analysis. He, too, has confronted frustration. "The French won't fund this because they say they're not responsible, and the Americans won't because they are," Adanhaim says.

International funding to Vietnam for ecological assistance, as with medical assistance, has been negligible. Kevin Bowen, a U.S. scientist familiar with the situation, thinks that assistance would dramatically increase if America reestablished diplomatic relations with Vietnam.

In American recognition, both diplomatic and a more heartfelt recognition of our responsibility to the citizens of Vietnam, lies the answer to the Agent Orange dilemma. The second need not wait for the first.

EXAMINING COUNTERPOINTS

This activity may be used as an individual study guide for students in libraries and resource centers or as a discussion catalyst in small group and classroom discussions.

The Point

On balance, the untoward effects of the herbicide program on the health of the South Vietnamese people appear to have been smaller than one might have feared. As was the case with humans, the effects of the herbicide spraying program on land and vegetation were also less than some scientists had suspected. Since the herbicides disappeared quickly in the soil, they had no significant effects on plants during the next growing season. (William Buckingham, Jr., *Operation Ranch Hand,* 1982.)

The Counterpoint

In addition to destroying trees and brush, in time these herbicides changed the composition of the soil, killing microorganisms, turning once fecund land infertile, and interrupting the natural cycle of succeeding species. In some areas, the dioxin persisted in the soil and nothing was able to grow up to ten years after the spraying. Vietnamese physicians connect a number of health problems to the dioxin in the blood of their citizens. Liver cancer, soft tissue cancer, lymphoma, and lung cancer have all been cited in studies. (Peter Korn, *The Amicus Journal*, Winter 1990.)

Guidelines

Social issues are usually complex, but often problems become oversimplified in political debates and discussion. Usually a polarized version of social conflict does not adequately represent the diversity of views that surround social conflicts.

1. Examine the counterpoints above. Then write down other possible interpretations of this issue than the two arguments stated in the counterpoints above.

CHAPTER 4

THE BIOLOGICAL WEAPONS DEBATE

THE BIOLOGICAL WEAPONS DEBATE

BIOLOGICAL RESEARCH PROGRAM IS NOT SAFE OR PRACTICAL

Jay A. Jacobson

Jay Jacobson is a physician specializing in infectious diseases and medical epidemiology and serves on the faculty at the University of Utah. His research interests include toxigenic infections and vaccine-preventable diseases. In the following article he discusses the high risks and minimal benefits of biological warfare research by the U.S. Army.

Points to Consider:

1. Who is the "natural enemy" referred to by the author?

2. What are the six reasons given for curtailing biological warfare research? Describe each in one or two sentences.

3. How does the author use the AIDS crisis as an analogy?

4. Try to describe your own hypothetical scenario involving a biological research accident.

Excerpted from testimony by Jay A. Jacobson before the House Subcommittee on Arms Control, International Security and Science of the Committee on Foreign Affairs, May 3, 1988.

Biological warfare research is inappropriately expensive. The proposed five-year modernization program at Dugway alone is to cost more than $300 million.

The Enemy

Since the mid-19th century when Pasteur, Koch and others first identified some of our microbial enemies, we have engaged in a continuing struggle. Our weapons against microbes have been improved. They include sanitation, aseptic technique, antibiotics and vaccines. We have won several battles. We have vanquished smallpox and nearly eliminated measles, polio, diphtheria, tetanus and whooping cough in our country and some parts of the world, but we have not won the war. Some agents have eluded our surveillance until very recently when we recognized their role in Legionnaires Disease and Toxic Shock Syndrome. Some such as HIV (Human Immunodeficiency Virus), the cause of AIDS, have only recently emerged as major threats to public health. Our biological enemies are highly adaptable, seemingly able to parry when we thrust our chemical swords at them. Staphylococci, initially vulnerable to treatment with penicillin became resistant to it and are now becoming resistant to more potent agents necessitating the use of very expensive and potentially dangerous antibiotics. Some bacteria have appeared which are resistant to virtually all of our antimicrobial drugs.

The enemy with which we are engaged is our natural enemy. It consists of viruses, bacteria, fungi, and parasites living out their life cycles which sometimes require injury to man and sometimes accidentally result in great harm to the human host as he or she attempts to imprison or repel these invaders.

The great havoc that infectious diseases can wreak and the fear that they engender has not gone unnoticed by military weapons strategists. New techniques in molecular biology and recombinant DNA technology now make it possible not only to use existing pathogens, our natural enemies, but also to create an infinite variety of new and tailor-made microbes, for the purpose of deliberately infecting, disabling or killing soldiers and civilians.

I will present six reasons why our defense department should not participate in efforts which increase the likelihood of deliberate biological warfare or an accidental biological attack on our own population or innocent global bystanders.

THE EDUCATION PRESIDENT — KIRK ©89

A theme that will permeate my remarks is that of risk and benefit. In the context of biological warfare research, the risk of a particular adverse event occurring may be small, but the consequences catastrophic. The benefits achieved may be theoretically very appealing, but the likelihood of achieving them is abysmally small.

Research Too Expensive

First, biological warfare research is inappropriately expensive. According to one source the budget for chemical and biological warfare research has risen from $18 million in 1980 to $90 million in 1986 and according to another it rose from $160 million to $1 billion in the same period. The proposed five-year modernization program at Dugway alone is to cost more than $300 million.

It is not at all clear to me what significant advances have been made as a result of this enormous expense. If all that is forthcoming is an improved mask or protective clothing which cannot be worn longer than several hours, I believe the investment has been a poor one and would predict no better return on the millions yet to be spent.

The risk is diversion of support from other more important, more worthy, and more solvable problems. The benefits to date have been trivial.

Research May Be Illegal

Second, proposed biological warfare research may be illegal. We signed a 1972 treaty which bans the development or stockpiling of biological warfare agents. Senator James Sasser has written to former Secretary of Defense Weinberger that the expanded facility at Dugway could be used "to test offensive biological and toxin weapons, a capability which is prohibited by the 1972 treaty." The military describes their research program on biological warfare as defensive and compatible with our obligations under the treaty. The projects are offensive to those of us who work toward the elimination rather than the creation of infectious diseases. They are likely to be construed as offensive by our political enemies and for understandable reasons.

The Army has insisted that it will be necessary to use real, virulent microorganisms under field conditions. This means they must test the enemies' present weapons, future weapons and anticipated weapons. This logically leads to the need to actually develop these biological weapons, use them and study their success or failure in overcoming defensive equipment. This weapons development is certainly in violation of the spirit if not the letter of the 1972 treaty and will inevitably lead to an escalation of overt or clandestine offensive research by others.

The risks here are to increase rather than decrease the development of biological warfare agents and to promote the creation of those that are harder to detect, harder to protect against and harder to treat.

Defense Is Futile

Third, the plethora of real and constructible microbial pathogens and the numerous ways in which exposure to them can occur makes development of defenses foolish and futile. For example, infection can be acquired through the air, from water and food, from animals, insects, and even other people. It can result from contamination of the soil. The microbes that can be used as weapons are not just the hundreds that are known to produce serious disease but uncountable numbers that can be constructed to live longer, to be more lethal, to be resistant to conventional treatment, to be more transmissible or even to wear microbial camouflage. This "wolf in sheep's clothing" concept is now feasible by inserting a lethal toxin-producing gene into otherwise harmless bacteria. This same technology has already been used for our benefit by having a yeast genetically reprogrammed to manufacture a part of the hepatitis B virus which is used in a vaccine.

A very grim scenario, indeed, would occur whereby individuals infected by any route could at least temporarily serve as asymptomatic transmitters of infection to companions or health care personnel. No one device or reasonable combination of devices is likely to detect and protect against all the various threats that can be mounted. The protective benefits of biological warfare defensive research are unlikely to be realized.

Defense Is Unnecessary

Fourth, developing so-called defenses against biological warfare seems not only expensive, politically dangerous and futile, but also unnecessary. Once man had the rifle, a leather shield against arrows became obsolete. There is no requirement that a defense must be specific or somehow symmetrical with an offensive weapon. There are, in fact, many weapons for which we have no specific individual defenses such as hand grenades or napalm. What we attempt to do is thwart their delivery by attacking soldiers and destroying airplanes. We have no lack of anti-personnel, anti-battalion, anti-airbase or anti-city weapons of the so-called conventional or nuclear type. Our ability to prevent the launching of a biological attack is extensive and our means for retaliating overwhelming. There is no particular advantage in biological warfare parity since the threat of biological counter attack is no greater than that of nuclear devastation or conventional conflict. If potential benefits are unnecessary or redundant, no cost and no level of risk is justified.

Research Is Dangerous

Fifth, biological warfare research is dangerous. It is hazardous to the health of those who do it, those who live with them, and potentially to all of us. Pathogenic microbes are dangerous. They produce disease and death. Those who work with them are exposed to risk just as those who work with explosives and radio-active material are. Accidents happen despite the most well-meaning, most conscientious, most well-monitored, most expensive and extensive precautions that can be taken. Witness, in our country, the space shuttle disaster, the accident at Three Mile Island. Witness, in the Soviet Union, the Chernobyl catastrophe. You realize that accident prevention and risk control programs were operating in all of those cases and you know that the planners calculated the risk of such accidents to be negligible. We continue to pursue development in nuclear power and space exploration because we believe the benefits outweigh the risks.

Test Results Kept from Public

Sixth, can the Army be relied on to keep their promises to perform only the tests they outline, to test only the pathogens they list in public documents? Historically, they have done little to inform the public about potentially dangerous tests and when testing went awry or the unexpected happened, they have been obstinate in releasing facts or acknowledging responsibility. Witness the fallout, radioactive and medical, from atomic bomb testing in Nevada and the massive sheep kill in Utah. In fairness, can we ask them to be honest with us when we mandate them to develop devices which necessitate the use of new deadly biological agents and acknowledge that their efforts can only be successful if they maintain complete secrecy from our enemies? I don't expect truth or open disclosure.

Summary

To summarize my concerns about biological warfare research, even "defensive" research: it is expensive, probably illegal, futile, unnecessary, dangerous, and necessarily secret.

My suggestion is to set aside biological warfare research, negotiate an even stronger treaty which is more comprehensive and which includes inspection and verification.

THE BIOLOGICAL WEAPONS DEBATE

BIOLOGICAL RESEARCH PROGRAMS ARE SAFE

Thomas J. Welch, Ph.D.

Dr. Thomas Welch is Deputy Assistant to the Secretary of Defense for Chemical Matters. In this statement Dr. Welch argues that the U.S. conducts no offensive biological warfare research and that the defensive programs are safe.

Points to Consider:

1. How is safety stressed by the Department of Defense in its chemical and biological research programs?

2. Explain the multi-tiered barrier system employed by Yale University.

3. What is the Department of Defense attitude toward safety inspections?

Excerpted from testimony by Thomas J. Welch before the Senate Committee on Governmental Affairs, July 27-28, 1988.

The Army applies stringent safety, storage, maintenance, use and accounting requirements for all internal and contractor facilities that use chemical agents.

At the outset, I would like to emphasize the Department of Defense (DOD) does not conduct any research and development related to offensive biological warfare; we have no biological warfare capabilities or programs. We are in strict compliance with the Biological and Toxin Weapon Convention and U.S. national policy. Our biological defense research program is conducted solely to enhance our ability to protect and defend the men and women of our armed services from the very real and worldwide threat of biological warfare.

Safety Stressed

There are potential safety risks to research personnel, the workplace and to the environment associated with conducting the research programs. To ensure safety of these DOD funded programs, both in-house and by contract, we have systems in place which effectively combine risk analyses, evaluations and inspections to minimize these risks.

The Army, as the responsible DOD Agency, applies stringent safety, storage, maintenance, use and accounting requirements for all internal and contractor facilities that use chemical agents. These are elaborated in Army regulation 50-6. Facilities, equipment and procedures are subject to continuous formal and informal inspection and review—both announced and unannounced—and to rehearsal of actions taken in response to hypothetical accidents. These inspections and reviews serve to assure that the combined facility, equipment and procedures are effective. In response to a study of Army chemical safety programs by the Department of the Army Inspector General, the Army Safety Office is drafting a comprehensive Army regulation on chemical safety. The Director of Army Safety and Commanders of Army research organizations have been directed to enhance their oversight and management of chemical safety programs.

It is appropriate to emphasize that the DOD's stringent and necessary safety precautions for chemical operations supplement other applicable federal, state and local safety requirements. While the focus of the Department's chemical safety programs

77

has been on insuring compliance with DOD requirements, institutional safety offices are responsible for assuring that these other applicable safety requirements are also met.

Improvement and Inspection

Finally, our system of continuous review of the adequacy of our regulations and management practices has resulted in constant improvement of our process.

Concerning regular safety inspections of chemical research facilities by agencies outside of DOD, we believe that a more practical approach would be for the Department to consult with other qualified Federal agencies. The Department would modify existing safeguards/controls where necessary to accommodate agreed upon recommendations. DOD would continue to inspect safety of Army and other services and contractor activities using the agreed upon safety inspection procedures. This approach is consistent with that used in other DOD programs and avoids statutory and regulatory conflicts within these essential national defense programs.

Biological Defense Research Program

The risks and safety precautions of the Biological Defense Research Program (BDRP) have been extensively addressed in the Draft Programmatic Environmental Impact Statement, Biological Defense Research Program, May 1988, and at public hearings. Handling of highly infectious, pathogenic or exotic organisms and toxins poses a potential risk to laboratory personnel, the workplace and the environment. Thus biosafety facilities, specialized procedures and safety equipment, as well as occupational health programs, have been developed to minimize these risks. Like all DOD funded research, the biological defense research program must comply with applicable Federal, state and local laws and regulations. This Subcommittee's Preliminary Report, 11 May 1988, identified that DOD expects, but does not require, adherence to the CDC-NIH (Center for Disease Control-National Institute of Health) Guidelines, "Biosafety in Microbiological Laboratories". Responding to that report, DOD directed that all aspects of the Biological Defense Research program — both in-house and contract — comply with these CDC-NIH Guidelines. In addition, senior Army leadership directed that the Army Safety Office develop an Army Regulation on Biological Defense Research Safety. This regulation is being drafted at this time.

While the Department would not oppose regular safety inspection of DOD sponsored biological defense research facilities by another qualified Federal Agency, in addition to those which already have access to our facilities, the merit of such inspections is not readily apparent.

It must be recognized that the facilities, special safety equipment and practices which are contained in the Center for Disease Control-National Institutes of Health Guidelines, "Biosafety in Microbiological Laboratories", evolved from those developed by the Army, the National Institutes of Health and the Center for Disease Control. These organizations continue to work together to enhance the safety of biological defense research.

In conclusion, the Department will continue to be uncompromising in maintaining safety and security standards in chemical warfare and chemical/biological defense research programs. We recognize our responsibility to keep Congress and the American public informed, especially of those programs that involve the safety of American citizens and the environment.

11 THE BIOLOGICAL WEAPONS DEBATE

ALL RESEARCH PROGRAMS ARE OFFENSIVE

Jonathan King

Jonathan King is Professor of Molecular Biology at the Massachusetts Institute of Technology in Cambridge, Massachusetts, where he teaches and researches genes and proteins of a group of viruses that infect bacteria. He also chairs the Committee on the Military Use of Biomedical Research of the Council of Responsible Genetics.

Points to Consider:

1. How do defensive and offensive uses of biotechnology overlap?

2. Discuss the threat of proliferation as a result of "defensive" research.

3. How does "defensive" research threaten our health and environment?

Excerpted from testimony by Jonathan King before the Senate Committee on Governmental Affairs, May 17, 1989.

The danger to us is not the development of biological weapons: it is the proliferation of biological weapons defense programs themselves.

Living organisms are qualitatively different from gunpowder, mustard gas and nuclear bombs. These agents, dangerous as they may be, do not grow and reproduce themselves. As a result of this fundamental feature of living creatures, they always have the potential to spread through populations and ecosystems, a feature of virus infections so tragically familiar to us at present. As a result, though always a hazard to human populations, they have never been effective weapons. It is particularly important to recognize that infectious agents recognize neither national boundaries nor uniforms, whether the black plague in the 14th century or AIDS in the 20th century.

It is not all clear that it will be possible using biotechnology to generate infectious agents that have the character of weapons: agents that will in a controlled manner cause damage to enemies and not to friends. However, I have no doubt that research efforts in this area will generate as side products organisms deleterious to the health and welfare of human plant and animal populations.

The danger to us is not the development of biological weapons: it is the proliferation of biological weapons defense programs themselves.

Overlap Between Defensive and Offensive

The self-reproducing character of living organisms, and the ever present potential for spread through a population, requires that any plan for offensive use begin with the ability to defend one's own troops or population.

Consider the development of a vaccine against a virus. Historically vaccines were made from inactivated viruses, so that preparation of the vaccines required growth of the virus in substantial quantities. With advances in biotechnology it is in many—though not all cases—possible to develop vaccines using only parts of the virus. However, sooner or later the vaccine must be tested. This means infecting animals or humans with the actual virulent form of the agent that you believe will be deployed. Thus intrinsic to any program is the gathering of data on the infectious properties of the weapon agent; the dosage required; the time course of the infection; its severity or degree

Neighborhood crime

of debilitation. Without such information it is impossible to evaluate the efficacy of the vaccine and carry out the primary mission.

Therefore, no matter how vigorously one proclaims or believes in the defensive intent, an informed observer knows that the data and technical capacity needed for the offensive side are always present.

This inability to separate offensive from defensive capacity is an intrinsic aspect of the Biological Defense Research Program (BDRP). It is not a flaw in the program, but follows inexorably from the fact that organisms are self-reproducing and

---

A TERRORIST'S DREAM

Millions of people would be infected if one or two litres of anthrax spores were let loose in the underground train networks of New York, Paris, Berlin or Frankfurt. Medical aid is possible. But the panic after such an attack and the sheer scale of the sickness would be an enormous strain on the best equipped civil catastrophe systems such as those in Germany.

Karl-Heinz Karisch, **The German Tribune**, Feb. 3, 1991

---

qualitatively different from other materials. No reorganization of the program can eliminate this problem.

Threat of Proliferation

Because of the ambiguous character of BDRP programs, they are provocative with respect to other nations, and destablizing with respect to the treaty regime. I'm sure the U.S. Department of Defense would not look favorably on the establishment of aerosol test facilities in Cuba, Nicaragua, Angola or the Soviet Union. The direct consequence of this can only be proliferation of such efforts by other nations around the globe.

However, even without this bimodality, the impetus for proliferation is equally great. After all, if these are really only defensive programs, and potentially efficacious against threat, why shouldn't other nations have them? Why shouldn't Pakistan and India have BDRP programs? Or Syria and Israel, Iran and Iraq, Honduras and Nicaragua?

Consider the consequences. In each case the mission will be to try to figure out beforehand what sort of novel pathogens the adversary may want to develop. Then to establish research programs on generating such novel pathogens so as to be able to prepare defenses.

We have enough problems trying to deal with scourges such as AIDS without catalyzing the growth around the world of investments designed to generate novel pathogens. Such a development would be a human tragedy of historic proportions.

The Question of Terrorism

The scale of equipment, materials and facilities required to carry out a full scale research program on infectious agents is far smaller than that required, for example, for ballistic missile development. Nonetheless, given the complexities of living organisms and the current state of knowledge, a program whose goal was to develop biological warfare agents is a major research project. Such agents would have many stringent requirements in terms of infectivity, survivability, transmissibility, storage properties, resistance to prophylaxis, etc.

Such a program requires many, many years of work by a relatively large group of highly trained scientists who would have to have access to modern technology in genetic engineering, instrumentation, enzymes, high powered computers, animal facilities, etc. A large library is required with continued access to current scientific journals.

In my estimation there is no possibility that such a program could be carried out by a terrorist group. If it was launched, it could not be kept hidden. Of course, such programs certainly can be initiated by the governments of many nations, as suggested above.

The danger from terrorists is not the development of biological weapons, but rather a raid on such a facility. Therefore, protection from terrorism again lies in the direction of strengthening the treaty and prohibiting the establishment of biological research for military purposes.

Health and Environmental Risks

The development of "defensive" biological weapons programs constitutes a substantial environmental and health risk to the nation conducting the research. As noted above, such programs generally require growing and testing agents thought to be related to potential biological war (BW) agents. Many of these will be pathogens or relatives of them. Even in the absence of an accident, it will be extremely difficult to develop and test the effects of such agents on organisms without substantial risk of their escape into the ecosystem.

Once a pathogen has entered the ecosystem, it may persist for long periods of time, causing significant disruption to the economy and/or public health of the area. For example, *Bacillus anthracis,* the bacterium responsible for anthrax, appears to be capable of establishing itself in a wide range of climates. This could lead to the creation of new and permanent reservoirs of the disease. A pathogen that has escaped into the environment has the potential to disperse by natural forces such as by wind, water or insect vectors. The survival and dispersal properties of such micro-organisms are difficult to predict or control.

Eliminate Weapons Program

Where does National Security lie in the long run? The Council of Responsible Genetics (CRG) believes that we should follow the path begun by President Nixon when he unilaterally terminated the U.S. BW program. This paved the way for the Biological Weapons Convention, the strongest multilateral disarmament treaty in modern history. The next step for U.S. policy is clearly to:

1. Terminate the BDRP and the Dugway test program. Transfer the funding for medically or technically useful aspects of the programs to civilian agencies to carry forward the scientifically useful aspects of the project.

2. Launch a Diplomatic Offensive publicizing the Biological Weapons Convention domestically and internationally. One rarely hears of this treaty from our own government agencies. The current issue of *Biotechnology* magazine with broad circulation carries a DOD sponsored report discussing military applications of biotechnology which makes no mention of the existence of such a treaty.

Our nation has been the world leader in the historic breakthrough in genetic engineering and biotechnology. We are now seeing the onset of a dangerous and tragic turn toward militarizing this technology. We should turn away and become the world leader in its peaceful development.

12 THE BIOLOGICAL WEAPONS DEBATE

THE U.S. HAS A DEFENSIVE PROGRAM

Matthew Meselson, Ph.D.

Matthew Meselson is Professor of Biochemistry and Molecular Biology at Harvard University. In the following statement, Meselson discusses the Biological and Toxic Weapons Convention of 1972 and the need for limited defensive biological research.

Points to Consider:

1. Why did the U.S. destroy its stockpile of offensive biological and toxic weapons?

2. What is our most important form of defense against biological and toxic weapons?

3. How can openness help in the research of biological weapons?

Excerpted from testimony by Matthew Meselson before the Senate Committee on Governmental Affairs, May 17, 1989.

I believe that there are areas of biological research in which the military should be engaged. These must be judged on a case-by-case basis.

Twenty years ago, after intensive interagency review, the United States unilaterally and unconditionally renounced the development and possession of biological and toxin weapons. Our considerable stockpiles of such weapons were destroyed and the facilities for developing and producing them were converted to other uses.

These U.S. decisions went far beyond the mere cancellation of a program. They renounced, without prior conditions, even the option to develop or acquire biological and toxin weapons. Why?

First, it was understood that biological weapons could be as great a threat to large populations as nuclear weapons and that no reliable defense is likely. Already having nuclear weapons, the U.S. has no need for an additional, less predictable, less targetable strategic system ineffective against hardened military installations.

Second, it was evident that biological weapons could be much simpler and less expensive than nuclear weapons to develop and produce. Proliferation of biological weapons would greatly increase the number of nations to which the populations of the United States and its allies are hostage.

Third, it was realized that our biological weapons program was pioneering an easily duplicated technology and that our program was likely to inspire others to follow suit.

The Convention of 1972

This stark analysis led to the conclusion that our biological weapons program was a substantial threat to our own security. The policy implication was that we should convincingly renounce biological weapons and seek to strengthen international barriers to their proliferation. In implementing this overall policy, the U.S. sponsored the Biological and Toxin Weapons Convention of 1972, ratified it in 1975 and led efforts to enhance the limited verification provisions of the Convention at its Second Review Conference in 1987.

Today, to the best of my knowledge, no nation possesses a stockpile of biological or toxin weapons. Nevertheless, there is

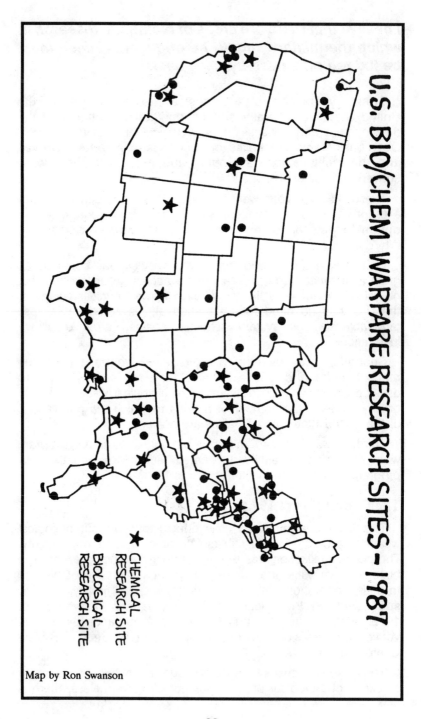

U.S. BIO/CHEM WARFARE RESEARCH SITES – 1987

★ CHEMICAL RESEARCH SITE

● BIOLOGICAL RESEARCH SITE

Map by Ron Swanson

justifiable concern that the recent proliferation and use of chemical weapons, particularly in the Middle East, may set the stage for attempts to develop and produce biological weapons.

The potential linkage between chemical and biological weapons is one of the factors that argues for pressing forward with our commitment to achieve a verifiable international ban on chemical weapons. This treaty, the Chemical Weapons Convention, is now in an advanced phase of negotiation by the 40-nation Committee on Disarmament in Geneva.

Defensive Research

Our first and most important line of defense against biological and toxin weapons is the effort to prevent their introduction into the arsenals of the world. We do this through our own example, through a growing and increasingly intrusive system of arms-control agreements, and by a variety of diplomatic activities backed up by the influence and prestige of the U.S.

In addition to these efforts to prevent the proliferation of biological and toxin weapons, there is the possibility of providing a limited defense against them. President Nixon in 1969 did not reject biological research for protective purposes. Instead, he announced that "We shall restrict our biological program to research for defensive purposes, strictly defined—such as techniques of immunization, safety measures and the control and prevention of the spread of disease."

This careful statement remains a good definition to guide U.S. military biological research programs. It subordinates biological research to the fundamental U.S. policy of renouncing biological weapons and building constraints against their proliferation. Moreover, it recognizes the requirement that our renunciation be convincing to others.

I recall that shortly after President Nixon's decisions, the White House sent inquiries to a considerable number of scientists and others who had been involved in the U.S. biological weapons program. The inquiry asked if the U.S. biological research program could be conducted without secrecy. The great majority of respondents replied that secrecy was not needed.

Openness in all biological research has advantages that far outweigh any risk. It makes U.S. policy credible. It helps in recruiting and keeping the most talented investigators and in exposing shoddy work or misguided lines of research. Openness accelerates progress through the kind of scientific interchange characteristic of the health sciences. Finally, by minimizing mutual suspicions, openness makes it possible for more nations to coordinate their efforts to combat disease and to guard against infringements of the prohibition of biological and toxin weapons.

Some Research Needed

I believe that there are areas of biological research in which the military should be engaged. These must be judged on a case-by-case basis. Military research should be done with the same high degree of openness that characterizes other research in medicine and public health. There should be meaningful civilian involvement in the oversight of the entire program, although it must also be recognized that the military has special needs for protection against hazards that the civilian sector tends to ignore. Organized and directed properly, military facilities can increasingly be used to enhance confidence in biological disarmament and to help overcome the very real threat to the military and to all mankind from naturally occurring disease.

13   THE BIOLOGICAL WEAPONS DEBATE

THE BIOLOGICAL WARFARE PROGRAM SHOULD BE ABOLISHED

Anthony Robbins, M.D.

Anthony Robbins is Professor of Public Health at the Boston University School of Public Health and past president of the American Public Health Association. In his statement which follows, Dr. Robbins presents reasons for halting all biological warfare testing.

Points to Consider:

1. The author describes a new and strictly hypothetical AIDS virus. Why does he do this?

2. What are the sources of danger from biological weapons research?

3. Discuss the three reasons put forth by the author for halting all such testing.

Excerpted from testimony by Anthony Robbins before the House Subcommittee on Arms Control, International Security and Science of the Committee on Foreign Affairs, May 3, 1988.

Today the number of potential agents has multiplied to the point where it is no longer possible to plan or respond with defenses.

On behalf of the American Public Health Association and the 35,000 public health professionals that make up its membership, I urge the Congress to recognize that modern biological weapons offer no reasonable opportunity for prevention and control. Public health measures have always been considered the basic defense against biological weapons. Ordinarily, prevention and control of biological agents are achieved by protective clothing, specific vaccines against the organisms and toxins, and specific drugs. However, weapons designed and built with modern biotechnology will leave us no reasonable opportunity to protect the public. This is true whether the public is exposed by military attack, by accident, or by terrorism.

The American Public Health Association (APHA) has twice adopted policy statements on biological warfare, the first in 1969 when President Nixon unilaterally renounced these methods and ordered the destruction of existing U.S. stockpiles, and again in 1974, just prior to the Senate's ultimate ratification of the Biological Warfare Convention which legally obligated this country to cease the development, production, and stockpiling of biological weapons. On each occasion APHA took note of the possibility that such weapons, however limited their tactical use, could cause unforeseen and uncontrollable public health and ecological effects.

Nothing has occurred in the meantime to mitigate these concerns. On the contrary, advances in genetic engineering and other new techniques of biotechnology have magnified both the theoretical lethal abilities of agents and their potential to create public health catastrophes. As the AIDS epidemic reminds us so forcefully, the great advances in controlling epidemic infectious diseases may be inadequate to cope with a novel microorganism. Recall that more people have died from malaria in this century than on all the battlefields in human history.

A Chilling Scenario

To illustrate the kind of hazard we might face if military researchers are able to modify the disease-causing potential of an organism by transferring genetic information from another organism, I have dreamed up a new and strictly hypothetical

AIDS virus. This example can illustrate how biological warfare agents might get beyond any control. As a starting point you should understand that AIDS, which may destroy a large part of the urban population of Africa, as well as smaller portions of the U.S., Europe, Asia and Latin America populace before it is controlled, is highly controllable compared to what could be created by biotechnology. Only a small percentage of sexual acts result in transmission of HIV from the infected individual to an uninfected individual. Transmission by blood is more efficient, but still only occurs in a minority of exposures. Because of the slow course of the epidemic, we have had over five years to change behavior and develop a preventive or curative vaccine or drug. Yet no vaccine has been effective and, in fact, a conventional vaccine may be impossible against HIV. And no drug has cured an AIDS patient or blocked transmission of the virus.

Now imagine a hypothetical new HIV as contagious as measles—which still kills more children in the world than AIDS. It is possible, for example, for your child to visit a doctor's office where another child was seen shortly before. The other child develops the classic signs of measles the next day. Your child, even without direct contact, was exposed to the measles virus and may develop the disease two weeks later. If today's HIV were as infectious as measles, the devastation from AIDS in the world might already be beyond repair.

Yet this is exactly the capacity of modern biology. It is possible to merge the characteristics of different organisms in a single new organism. We are thrilled when the *vaccinia* virus, which was used for smallpox vaccinations, can be engineered to immunize against six diseases at the same time, but we should be terrified that other viruses can be made highly infectious, highly virulent, and highly toxic.

The Sources of Danger

Everyone knows that biological weapons are dangerous. That is why they are designed and built. But what are the sources of these dangerous organisms that worry public health officials? The first is military testing, which is being considered here today. Testing, even for defense, means our country will develop biological warfare agents here in the U.S. As explained to me, the main strategy for defense against biological weapons is to invent, design, and build all of the organisms that an opponent might be building to use against us, and then to create specific defenses, such as vaccines. Even if this were possible, and few believe it is, it would mean that we would be using and storing within the United States the very organisms that we and our enemies agree would be good weapons.

The second source is incomplete. The new biotechnology industry is experimenting with vectors. Vectors are simply the infectious agents capable of transferring genetic material and information to other organisms. Vectors are essential to biotechnology and an important element in building biological weapons. Thus elements of biological weapons are increasingly available in industry. Industry might also represent a source of more complete biological agents if the Defense Department contracts with biotechnology firms to develop these agents. The hazard is then magnified because most of the new biotechnology firms are located in populated areas around universities and near Boston, San Francisco and Washington.

Finally, we could be exposed to biological weapons by terrorists.

Although biotechnology is very sophisticated and demands great brain power, it is still "low technology." Many new organisms could be built in a kitchen and produced in great quantities in a brewery. It appears that a knowledgeable terrorist could produce biological weapons far more easily than nuclear weapons.

Defense Has Become Impossible

One cannot overstate our inability to deal with novel agents. In principle a scientist who has designed a new biological agent and produced it might also be able to produce a vaccine or drug against the new organism. But for unprepared public health authorities who know nothing of the weapon organism's structure, pathogenic mechanisms, and transmission, the task of producing a vaccine or drug, and doing it very rapidly, is almost impossible.

There was a time when microbiologists could catalogue in a few pages the organisms and toxins that were most likely to be used as weapons. Today the number of potential agents has multiplied to the point where it is no longer possible to plan or respond with defenses. Defense of populations against new biological weapons is no longer possible. There is no public health or medical strategy.

Three Reasons for Halting Testing

The American Public Health Association believes that the United States must not engage in testing of biological warfare agents. Here are three reasons:

1. The United States has renounced biological weapons in a treaty. Although the treaty still needs a law to implement it, Secretary Weinberger stated as follows in 1984: "The United States does not and will not possess biological or toxin weapons. We will not develop such weapons nor assist others to do so."

2. As indicated above, the development of agents to test defenses is operationally equivalent to the development of agents for offense. Thus even if defense were possible, which it is not, it would be impossible to convince other nations that our testing activities are intended for protection of our population and not for attack.

3. Promises about safety measures should be highly suspect. It is hard to believe that any safety system is sufficient to cope with a biological agent that has been created in advance of any control or prevention method. The risks may approach the infinite, but I doubt the effectiveness of safety measures do. The goal in building biological warfare agents is to achieve uncontrollable spread, except for protected populations.

Chernobyl and Three Mile Island happened despite assurances about safety measures. But even the worst nuclear accident has a limited effect. Biological agents may spread death until the susceptible population is reduced to the point where the epidemic peters out.

14 THE BIOLOGICAL WEAPONS DEBATE

TOTAL OPENNESS NEEDED IN BIOLOGICAL WARFARE RESEARCH

James F. Leonard

James F. Leonard was the former Chief U.S. Negotiator at the Biological Weapons Convention of 1972. In the following statement he addresses the intent of the treaty that resulted from this convention and the need for openness in biological warfare research.

Points to Consider:

1. Discuss the "purpose criterion" of the treaty that resulted from the 1972 Weapons Convention.

2. Why is research in this area so ambiguous?

3. Why does the author feel that total openness is so crucial in any biological warfare research?

Excerpted from testimony by James F. Leonard before the House Subcommittee on Arms Control, International Security and Science of the Committee on Foreign Affairs, May 3, 1988.

It may sound radical and quite unrealistic, but I believe that in fact there are no activities relating to research on biological warfare which should be kept secret.

The Biological Weapons Convention (or treaty—the terms are interchangeable) became a practical possibility in 1971, when the Soviet Union dropped its resistance to our position that the problem of prohibiting possession of biological weapons should be separated from the problem of chemical weapons and should be negotiated first. We had been urging this since 1969 and our British allies had led the way even earlier.

Treaty Criteria

The problem of the criteria for distinguishing between what the treaty would permit and would prohibit had been a difficult one for us, both in our deliberations within the U.S. Government and in our discussions with our allies. I will not go through the alternatives that were rejected but will simply say that we had settled on what we called a "purpose criterion." We had agreed that despite the advantages of prohibiting all activity involving research on possible agents of biological warfare, it was essential to permit governments to do research and other activities relating to defense against biological warfare. Moreover, many potential agents are naturally occurring substances which humanity must study and improve its ability to deal with.

It was clear, therefore, that "objective" criteria such as the toxicity of agents or quantities of agents could not be used and that the only possible criterion was the "subjective" criterion of intent. Activities aimed at "prophylactic, protective or other peaceful purposes" are permitted. The possession of agents "of types and in quantities that have no justification" for these peaceful purposes is prohibited by Article I of the treaty, from which I have been quoting.

Research Not Clearly Defined

The use of the purpose criterion, though unavoidable and controversial, means that there is no ready yardstick, no scientific test, available to us to discriminate between what a government may and may not do under the treaty. The stockpiling of militarily significant quantities of any agent is clearly prohibited. That is what the treaty is about. But research is a more complicated matter and we have to ask what is the object, the intent of the research program. We can look at particular research activities and say that these "have no justification" or do have a justification, but these will be judgments on our part, not a matter of reading a dial that "proves" a conclusion beyond any dispute.

Total Openness

It may sound radical and quite unrealistic, but I believe that in fact there are no activities relating to research on biological warfare which should be kept secret, except intelligence studies. It is healthy, I believe, for other governments to be somewhat uncertain how much we know about their activities, but it is also healthy for us to deliberately make available to all qualified scientists everywhere the totality of the research that we are doing on defense against biological and toxin weapons. I have been told that some years ago a panel chaired by a distinguished expert in this area, Dr. Ivan Bennett, studied thoroughly the pros and cons of this question and reached the conclusion that I have just summarized.

I will conclude by noting that a careful reading of Article X of the treaty indicates to me that this "total openness" or "transparency" or "glasnost", if you will, is not only in our security interest but is in fact an obligation of parties to the treaty. I do not imagine that the Soviet Government will readily agree, but I recall that the Biological Weapons Treaty grew out of a unilateral renunciation of Biological Weapons by President Nixon in 1969. Moving toward complete transparency seems to me not only worth exploring with the Soviet Government but also worth considering as another act of unilateral American statesmanship and leadership.

15 THE BIOLOGICAL WEAPONS DEBATE

ENVIRONMENTAL IMPACT OF BIOLOGICAL WEAPONS RESEARCH

Jeremy Rifkin

Jeremy Rifkin is President of the Foundation on Economics Trends, a public interest organization which assesses the economic, environmental and ethical risks involved in emerging technologies. The Foundation, in 1984, brought a lawsuit challenging the U.S. Department of Defense on its plans to construct a biological warfare testing facility at Dugway, Utah.

Points to Consider:

1. How is biological warfare defined?

2. What are "designer" weapons?

3. What concerns are brought up when discussing biological warfare experiments?

4. What was the major objection to the proposed facility at Dugway, Utah?

5. How should the Army alter its Biological Warfare Testing Facility?

Excerpted from testimony by Jeremy Rifkin before the House Subcommittee on Arms Control, International Security and Science of the Committee on Foreign Affairs, May 3, 1988.

Genetic engineering can also be used to destroy specific strains of agricultural plants or domestic animals if the intent is to cripple the economy of a country.

Biological warfare involves the use of living organisms for military purposes. Biological weapons can be viral, bacterial, fungal, rickettsial and protozoan. They can be used to destroy animals, crops, and people. Biological agents can mutate, reproduce, multiply and spread over a large geographic terrain by wind, animal and insect transmission. Once released, many biological pathogens are capable of developing a viable niche and maintaining themselves in the environment indefinitely. Traditional biological agents include *Yersinia pestis* (the plague), tularemia, Rift Valley fever, *Coxiella burnetil* (Q fever), eastern equine encephalitis, and smallpox.

Biological warfare has never been widely used because of the expense and danger involved in processing and stockpiling large volumes of toxic materials, and the difficulty in targeting the dissemination of biological agents. However, new advances in genetic engineering technologies over the past decade have made biological warfare a viable possibility for the first time in history.

In a May 1986 report to the Committee on Appropriations of the United States House of Representatives, the Department of Defense pointed out that recombinant DNA and other genetic engineering technologies are finally making biological warfare an effective military option. Genetic engineers are cloning previously unattainable quantities of "traditional" pathogens. The technology can also be used to create "novel" pathogens never before seen.

Designer Weapons

Recombinant DNA "designer" weapons can be created in many ways. The new technologies can be used to program genes into infectious micro-organisms to increase their antibiotic resistance, virulence, and environmental stability. It is also possible to insert lethal genes into harmless micro-organisms resulting in biological agents that the body recognizes as friendly and does not resist. It is even possible to insert genes into organisms which affect regulatory functions that control mood and behavior, mental status, body temperature, and other functions. Scientists say they may be able to clone selective toxins to eliminate specific racial or ethnic groups whose genotypical make-up predisposes them to certain disease patterns. Genetic engineering can also be used to destroy specific strains of agricultural plants or domestic animals if the intent is to cripple the economy of a country. In recent months advances have been made in the creation of genetically engineered microbes which are designed to self-destruct after a given period of time. The implications of this, and other advances in genetic engineering, are extraordinary and frightening.

The new genetic engineering technologies provide a versatile form of weaponry that can be used for a wide variety of military purposes ranging from terrorism and counter-insurgency operations to large scale warfare aimed at entire populations. Unlike nuclear technologies, genetic engineering can be cheaply developed and produced, requires far less scientific expertise, and can be effectively employed in many more diverse settings.

The exponential growth of the Biological Defense Program (BDP) over the last seven years has the potential for significant adverse effects on the environment and public health. According to the Department of Defense (DOD), as of February 1988, biological warfare research is ongoing in more than 19 government labs, 50 non-governmental research labs and institutions, and over 85 colleges and universities. This research involves numerous bacteria strains such as *Salmonella marcescenes*, and *Yersina pestis,* numerous viruses including Rift Valley fever, yellow fever, poliovirus, Ebola and Marburg viruses and human retroviruses; and more than seventy toxins, including T2 mycotoxin, Scorpion toxin, and Mojave rattlesnake toxin. The BDP has also conducted over 75 recombinant DNA experiments.

Senator Orrin Hatch (R-Utah) has maintained that biological warfare experiments in populated areas constitute "reckless endangerment" and has advocated "a remote island for any future biotoxin work." The environmental impacts of this research bring up the following concerns: 1) effects on the general public from potential exposure to biological warfare agents during normal operations or due to advertent or inadvertent release of the hazardous organisms (i.e. human error, equipment failure, terrorism, or natural disasters); 2) effects on DOD personnel from potential exposure to biological warfare agents being researched; 3) impacts on air, and water quality and biota from BDP operations or accidents; 4) laboratory security; 5) risks involved in decontaminating facilities; 6) treatment and disposal of BDP research wastes; 7) transportation and shipping of BDP pathogens; and 8) economic and social impacts to areas adjoining BDP sites.

The Foundation on Economic Trends has embarked on a series of actions over the last 5 years which temporarily halted certain biological warfare research work, focused public attention on the military application of genetic engineering technology, and forced the Department of Defense to prepare environmental impact statements (EISs) on the health and environmental implication of the BDP.

The Dugway Controversy

In December 1984, the Foundation on Economic Trends, its President Jeremy Rifkin, and other plaintiffs filed a motion for a preliminary injunction to enjoin the construction of the proposed aerosol biological warfare testing facility (BATF) at Dugway, Utah. Plaintiffs maintained that the Army had not prepared an environmental assessment (EA) for the facility and were therefore not in compliance with the National Environmental Policy Act (NEPA). Approximately one month later, the Army released an EA for the BATF. Contending that the EA was grossly inadequate, plaintiffs quickly moved for a permanent injunction on the facility.

On May 31, 1985, Federal District Court Judge Joyce Hens Green permanently enjoined the construction of the lab citing the "serious and far-reaching risks" involved in its operation. Judge Green held that the EA was "clearly inadequate" and a "substantive violation" of NEPA.

As a result of the federal court order, the Army elected to prepare an Environmental Impact Statement for the Dugway facility (hereinafter "Dugway EIS"). After months of delay, the Dugway EIS was released in February 1988. A public hearing was scheduled for March 14, at Tooele, Utah.

The release of the Dugway EIS has led to considerable controversy in Utah. Scientists, environmentalists, and several elected officials, including the Governor, have spoken out against the construction of the lab in Utah and called for additional public hearings.

The form and content of an EIS must foster both informed decision-making and informed public participation. Crucial to

104

fulfilling this purpose is that an EIS "provide full and fair discussion of significant environmental impacts and. . .inform the decision makers and the public of the reasonable alternatives which would avoid or minimize adverse impacts."

In sum, the Dugway EIS is shoddily prepared, grossly inadequate, and in clear violation of NEPA and its relevant regulations. The Dugway EIS fails to adequately assess the risks of the construction and operation of the BATF and also fails to conduct a full discussion of possible alternatives. The EIS is virtually useless as a document to inform either decision makers or the public on the BATF.

The Foundation is organizing grass roots opposition in Utah to counter the construction of the Dugway facility. Furthermore, the Foundation will once again litigate to stop the DOD from building and using this hazardous facility.

Future Action

In order for the DOD to minimize the environmental impacts of its BDP program, it will have to significantly modify its implementation of the BDP program. This alteration would have to involve the change in the conduct, type and scale of BDP activities. The first step in improving the conduct of BDP activities would be mandatory compliance with the National Institute of Health (NIH) Guidelines, vastly improved security at BDP labs, and greater care taken to insure the safety of workers. Changes in BDP activities should include a total commitment to the use of simulants rather than the toxic materials currently in use. Reducing the scale of BDP would require maintaining a precise inventory of all BDP materials.

Finally, the environmental impacts of the BDP program could

be minimized through a change in the location of BDP operations. Such research should not be dispersed through the several dozen laboratories currently in use. Instead any BDP research found absolutely necessary should be located at remote sites away from populations.

RECOGNIZING AUTHOR'S POINT OF VIEW

This activity may be used as an individualized study guide for students in libraries and resource centers or as a discussion catalyst in small group and classroom discussions.

Many readers are unaware that written material usually expresses an opinion or bias. The capacity to recognize an author's point of view is an essential reading skill. The skill to read with insight and understanding involves the ability to detect different kinds of opinions or bias. **Sex bias, race bias, ethnocentric bias, political bias and religious bias** are five basic kinds of opinions expressed in editorials and all literature that attempts to persuade. They are briefly defined in the glossary below.

5 Kinds of Editorial Opinion or Bias

Sex Bias—the expression of dislike for and/or feeling of superiority over the opposite sex or a particular sexual minority

Race Bias—the expression of dislike for and/or feeling of superiority over a racial group

Ethnocentric Bias—the expression of a belief that one's own group, race, religion, culture or nation is superior. Ethnocentric persons judge others by their own standards and values.

Political Bias—the expression of political opinions and attitudes about domestic or foreign affairs

Religious Bias—the expression of a religious belief or attitude

Guidelines

1. Locate three examples of political opinion or bias in the readings from Chapter Four.

2. Locate five sentences that provide examples of any kind of editorial opinion or bias from the readings in Chapter Four.

3. Write down each of the above sentences and determine what kind of bias each sentence represents. Is it *sex bias, race bias, ethnocentric bias, political bias or religious bias?*

4. Make up one-sentence statements that would be an example of each of the following: *sex bias, race bias, ethnocentric bias, political bias and religious bias.*

5. See if you can locate five sentences that are factual statements from the readings in Chapter Four.

Summarize author's point of view in one sentence for each of the following readings:

Reading 9 _____

Reading 10 _____

Reading 11 _____

Reading 12 _____

Reading 13 _____

Reading 14 _____

Reading 15 _____

CHAPTER 5

HALTING THE SPREAD OF CHEMICAL WEAPONS

16   HALTING THE SPREAD OF CHEMICAL WEAPONS

CHEMICAL WEAPONS CONTROL: AN OVERVIEW

Steven R. Bowman

Steven Bowman is an analyst in national defense with the Foreign Affairs and National Defense Division of the U.S. Library of Congress.

Points to Consider:

1. How will the U.S. destroy its stockpiles of chemical weapons?

2. How will the Soviets destroy their stockpiles?

3. List the various on-going forums for the international control of chemical weapons. Have they been successful?

4. Describe the major hold-up in disarmament negotiations.

Excerpted from a report by Steven R. Bowman entitled "Chemical Weapons: U.S. Production, Destruction, and Arms Control Negotiations", The Library of Congress, March 13, 1991.

On June 1, 1990, the United States and the Soviet Union signed an agreement requiring each side to destroy 50 percent of its chemical weapons (CW) by 1999, and all but 5,000 metric tons by 2002. Each side also agreed to cease chemical weapons production when the agreement comes into force, probably in mid-1991. Both nations reaffirmed their support for the multilateral CW negotiations in Geneva, and pledged to destroy all but 500 tons of their stockpiles within 8 years of a global CW ban coming into effect.

The United States already has started a program to destroy the current stockpile of older munitions. Congress has directed that the unitary stockpile be destroyed by 1997, but this deadline may be modified owing to the U.S.-Soviet agreement and delays in starting up the Johnston Atoll destruction facility. The munitions will be destroyed in facilities to be constructed at each one of the current CW storage facilities. The pilot destruction facility at Johnson Atoll in the South Pacific has started initial operations. Shipment of the U.S. chemical munitions stockpile in Germany to Johnston Atoll for destruction has been completed.

Negotiations for a convention to ban globally the production, stockpiling, and use of chemical weapons continue at the Conference on Disarmament (CD) in Geneva. For the last two years, the CD negotiations have been marked by an increasingly accommodating attitude on the part of the Soviet Union, more active participation by Third World nations, and charges that the United States has not pursued negotiations with full vigor. Some attribute the cautious U.S. approach to doubts among some Bush Administration officials about verification and enforcement of a global CW ban.

Destroying Chemical Stockpiles

The CW destruction program continues to stimulate debate over competing technical approaches, while the pilot facility has experienced delays in operational testing. In Geneva, international efforts to ban chemical weapons enter their twenty-second year. A general atmosphere of optimism about arms control is tempered by the proliferation of chemical arsenals and concerns over the verification and enforcement of a global chemical weapons ban. Among the issues are: (1) What constitutes an adequate deterrent CW stockpile, pending completion of a CW convention? (2) What is the safest and most cost-effective means to destroy obsolete chemical

munitions? (3) Can a CW convention be adequately verified and enforced? (4) Should the United States retain a small CW stockpile until all CW-capable nations sign a convention?

Negotiations over specific verification and destruction procedures for the U.S.-Soviet CW agreement signed last June were to have been completed in December 1990. They have been prolonged, reportedly over the question of how much assistance the United States will provide the Soviet Union in destroying its chemical arsenal. The June 1990 agreement provided for destruction technology to be shared, but there is now speculation the Soviets are requesting financial assistance or U.S. participation in building facilities to meet the agreement's deadlines.

The Army is currently revising its cost estimates for the chemical weapons destruction program, with the highest estimates adding $2 billion to the previous estimate of $3.7 billion over the next 7-8 years. Army officials now also doubt that the April 30, 1997, deadline for destruction of the entire stockpile can be met. Delays in starting the operational testing of the Johnston Atoll destruction facility have set back the Army's original timetable. The Army anticipates further delays in building planned destruction facilities in the continental United States as it attempts to comply with increasingly exigent environmental concerns.

Congress required that the U.S. unitary chemical weapons stockpile be destroyed by 1997. To accomplish this, the Army prepared a destruction schedule that calls for the construction of destruction facilities at each of the current storage depots. One destruction plant has been completed at Johnston Atoll in the South Pacific, and a second is under construction at Tooele, Utah. Several factors, however, have now prompted Congress to call for a re-examination of the destruction program. First, the destruction schedule called for in the U.S.-Soviet bilateral CW agreement is not consistent with the 1997 deadline or the Army's destruction schedule. The bilateral agreement calls for each party to destroy 50 percent of their stockpiles by 1999, and all but 5,000 agent tons by 2002. The agreement also allows for postponement of these deadlines, should either party encounter delays in the destruction process.

Two different techniques for destroying the munitions have been under study. The Johnston Atoll facility uses the so-called "baseline" destruction process in which the munition is disassembled and its components are incinerated in four separate furnaces. A second approach, called "cryofracture," is in development. This technique freezes, crushes, and then incinerates each munition using one furnace. The Army found cryofracture to be cost-effective, but the Secretary of Defense deleted FY (fiscal year) 1990 funding for further development of the technique. In doing so, the Secretary cited confidence in the reliability of the baseline approach and concern that research and development on cryofracture would jeopardize meeting the congressionally-mandated deadline for unitary

113

munitions destruction. Congress disagreed with this assessment and appropriated $6.1 million for FY1990 to continue cryofracture development.

As CW destruction gets underway at Johnston Atoll, the Marshall Islands and Kiribati have objected to the transfer of munitions from West Germany to the South Pacific destruction facility. Demonstrations against the transfer have also been held in Hawaii by those who discount Army assurances, and fear that the Pacific is being used as a convenient "dumping ground" for hazardous materials. The Prime Ministers of Australia and New Zealand, however, have accepted the West German munitions transfer, though they caution against additional munitions being brought to Johnston for destruction.

Soviet Stockpiles

In accordance with a memorandum of understanding with the United States, signed September 1989, the Soviet Union has begun an exchange of detailed information on current CW stockpiles. This information remains classified. In general terms, the Soviets have acknowledged a total CW inventory of 50,000 metric tons. The Defense Intelligence Agency has placed the inventory at 75,000 tons, while the CIA believes Soviet stocks are actually under 50,000 tons.

In the spring of 1988, the Soviet Union declared it had ceased production of chemical weapons. It appears that Soviet CW destruction capabilities are severely limited. At the Canberra conference (September 1989) of government and private CW experts, Soviet representatives estimated the U.S.S.R. was 5 to 10 years behind the United States. Its newly built destruction facility at Chapayevsk was shut down almost immediately after it opened in response to public fears about environmental contamination. In hopes of improving Soviet capabilities, the United States has agreed to negotiate the provision of technology for the construction and operation of destruction facilities.

Conference on Disarmament

The Conference on Disarmament (CD) is an independent arm of the United Nations charged with negotiating disarmament agreements. Current CD member nations are: Algeria, Argentina, Australia, Belgium, Brazil, Bulgaria, Burma, Canada, China, Cuba, Czechoslovakia, Egypt, Ethiopia, East Germany,

France, Great Britain, Hungary, India, Indonesia, Iran, Italy, Japan, Kenya, Mexico, Mongolia, Morocco, Netherlands, Nigeria, Pakistan, Peru, Poland, Romania, Soviet Union, Sri Lanka, Sweden, United States, Venezuela, West Germany, Yugoslavia, and Zaire. In addition, the following CD non-member states have been invited to participate in the CW negotiations: Bangladesh, Denmark, Finland, Greece, Iraq, Ireland, Libya, New Zealand, North Korea, Norway, Portugal, Senegal, Spain, Switzerland, Syria, Tunisia, Turkey, and Zimbabwe.

Since 1968, the CD and predecessor organizations have carried on negotiations to ban chemical weapons. From 1976 to 1980, the United States and the Soviet Union conducted closed bilateral CW treaty negotiations without reaching an accord, and subsequently returned to the CD as their primary negotiating forum. Within the CD, the Chemical Weapons Ad Hoc Committee holds responsibility for drafting a convention banning the production, stockpiling, and use of chemical weapons world-wide.

Verification

Verification remains the major stumbling block. Current discussion centers on procedures for "challenge" inspections and "ad hoc" inspections. The United States has proposed that government facilities and private industrial facilities with government contracts be subject to challenge inspections. These inspections would be initiated within 24 hours of the executive body receiving a request. After years of resistance, the Soviet Union accepted the principle of challenge inspection, but has sought to extend it to all private facilities. The Soviets have pointed out that all Soviet industrial facilities are government-owned. Thus, the U.S. proposal would include all Soviet facilities and exclude the majority of U.S. (private) facilities. The acknowledged existence of U.S. classified "black" defense contracts also would complicate or prevent identification of facilities with government contracts.

International Activities

Australia Group — In response to an Australian initiative in 1984, member nations of the Organization for Economic Cooperation and Development (OECD) joined together to establish voluntary export controls on certain chemicals. The "Australia Group", an informal organization open to any nation seeking to stem CW proliferation, now has 20 member states:

the twelve members of the European Community plus Australia, Austria, Canada, Japan, New Zealand, Norway, Switzerland, and the United States. The Commission of the European Community is also a member. Each nation has established controls on the export of 40 chemicals deemed useful in the production of chemical weapons.

U.S.-Soviet Bilateral Consultations on Proliferation — At the 1985 Reagan-Gorbachev Summit meeting, the United States and the Soviet Union agreed to informally discuss CW proliferation. Soviet and U.S. representatives met three times (March 1986, September 1986, and October 1987) to discuss efforts to stem CW proliferation. The meetings were closed sessions, reportedly involving the exchange of intelligence information on proliferation and lists of chemicals to be placed under export controls. Though thought to be a useful channel of communication, these consultations have not reconciled U.S.-Soviet differences in perspective, as demonstrated in 1988 by the Soviet Foreign Minister Shervardnadze's refusal to accept U.S. evidence that the Libyan plant at Rabta is designed to produce chemical weapons. Nevertheless, during Secretary of State Baker's visit to Moscow in February 1990, he and Foreign Minister Shevardnadze pledged to intensify joint anti-proliferation cooperation.

United Nations — In 1989, the United Nations established a six-nation working group (the United States, Soviet Union, France, Sweden, Egypt, and Bulgaria) to draft a procedure to be followed by the UN Secretary-General for investigating suspected use of chemical and biological weapons. Currently, the Secretary-General may order an investigation at his discretion. The new procedure is expected to require the Secretary-General to order an investigation when presented an allegation by any member nation.

Paris Conference 1989 — On September 26, 1988, President Reagan, in addressing the United Nations General Assembly, called for a conference of the signatories of the 1925 Geneva Protocol, which banned the use of chemical and biological weapons in war. As the repository nation for the protocol, France hosted the conference and extended the invitation to all nations. Syria, Algeria, Egypt, and Iraq all defended the right to produce chemical weapons, citing them as a necessary counterbalance to the nuclear weapons of more developed nations, and calling for a linkage of chemical and nuclear disarmament.

17 HALTING THE SPREAD OF CHEMICAL WEAPONS

A TOTAL BAN ON CHEMICAL WEAPONS IS NEEDED

Lewis A. Dunn

Lewis A. Dunn, former Assistant Director of the Arms Control and Disarmament Agency is an Assistant Vice-President (Negotiations and Planning Division) of the Science Applications International Corporation in McLean, Virginia. Dr. Dunn has managed projects and conducted analyses on chemical and nuclear weapons as well as on-site inspection and treaty verification.

Points to Consider:

1. What problems would a total ban on chemical weapons pose with respect to verification?

2. Discuss the benefits of a total ban on chemical weapons.

3. How would the Soviet Union be involved?

4. Do you feel a total ban on chemical weapons could have brought international action against Iraq during its war with Iran?

Excerpted from testimony by Lewis A. Dunn before the Subcommittee on International Finance and Monetary Policy of the Committee on Banking, Housing, and Urban Affairs, June 22, 1989.

Assuming continued pursuit of a complete and total chemical weapons ban, measures can also be taken now and in the future to contain its risks for U.S. security.

Chemical weapons proliferation has risen to the top of the global security agenda. Chemical weapons were used repeatedly by Iraq in the Gulf War. Estimates by Administration spokesmen indicate that upwards of 20 Third World countries either possess, or are seeking to acquire chemical weapons. Many of these countries also are developing ballistic missiles that could be used for delivery.

In recent years, responses to this growing threat of chemical weapons proliferation have moved ahead on several different fronts. Progress has been made in the multilateral negotiations at the Geneva Conference on Disarmament on a complete and total ban on the acquisition, production, stockpiling, transfer, or use of chemical weapons. Under the framework of the Australia Group, supplier countries have sought to tighten export controls on chemicals. But as controversy over assistance by West German firms to Libya's Rabta chemical weapons plant demonstrated, the results of these suppliers' efforts have sometimes been mixed. Legislation has been introduced in both Houses of Congress to impose sanctions on firms that have assisted countries to acquire chemical weapons capabilities as well as on countries using these weapons.

During his election campaign, President Bush declared: "And if I'm elected President, if I'm remembered for anything, it would be this: a complete and total ban on chemical weapons." The Bush Administration—and the U.S. Congress—now face three difficult questions in dealing with the threat of chemical weapons proliferation:

First, should the United States, in light of growing concerns about its effective verification, retreat from the goal of a complete and total chemical weapons ban? Second, assuming a decision to stick to that goal—which I support—what steps can be taken now and in the future to contain its risks? Third, what measures can be adopted to strengthen international export controls in this field, as well as to establish a presumption that chemical weapons users will "pay a price"?

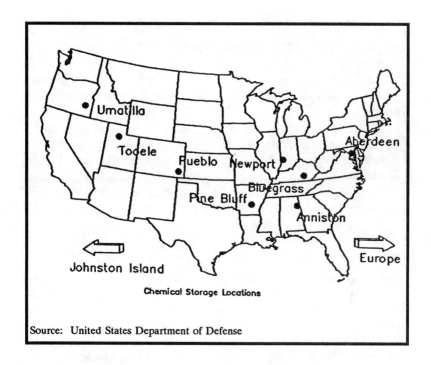

Umatilla

Tooele

Pueblo

Newport

Pine Bluff

Bluegrass

Anniston

Aberdeen

Johnston Island

Europe

Chemical Storage Locations

Source: United States Department of Defense

A Chemical Weapons Convention and Verification

Verification is widely acknowledged to be the potential Achilles heel of a complete and total chemical weapons ban. Even with extensive provisions for on-site inspection, uncertainties dominate the verification tally-sheet. In particular, monitoring civilian chemical industry facilities that use key precursor chemicals to detect misuse will be a demanding task. Detecting undeclared production of chemical weapons agents will be an even more formidable problem.

Continued improvement in the East-West political relationship, as well as a defensive restructuring of Soviet conventional forces in Europe, could reduce the risks to the United States of verification uncertainties.

Benefits of a Total Ban

Most important, the verification uncertainties and potential military risks of a complete and total ban must be weighed against the important benefits of such a ban for U.S. efforts to check the proliferation of chemical weapons to conflict-prone Third World regions. Among those benefits are:

119

First, international agreement to a legally binding ban on
development, acquisition, and use of chemical weapons would
promote renewed global support for non-use of chemical
weapons. As a result, fewer countries would think seriously
about the need for their own chemical weapons arsenal.

Second, successful negotiation and implementation of a
complete and total ban, with widespread adherence, would go
far to reverse the current perception that the increasingly
widespread proliferation of chemical weapons is unavoidable.
This, too, would lessen pressures to acquire such weapons.

Third, legally binding obligations under a chemical weapons
ban not to assist other countries to obtain chemical weapons
would greatly assist our efforts to strengthen multilateral export
controls and to ensure their effective implementation. One clear
lesson from over fifteen years of nuclear export controls is that
without such a legal foundation, U.S. and likeminded countries in
their attempts to strengthen export controls will face an uphill
battle.

Fourth, though important, export control efforts by themselves
can only buy time, slowing eventual acquisition of chemical
weapons capabilities by Third World countries. This, too, is a
lesson of nuclear export controls. A chemical weapons arms
control treaty offers a longer term, political approach to chemical
weapons proliferation.

NO EFFECTIVE RESPONSE

Chemical and biological weapons have the potential for immense destruction to human life and health and to the ecosystem on which our lives depend. Both types of weapons have characteristics that make them especially dangerous to human rights. These weapons are indiscriminate, affecting both combatants and non-combatants. For both types of weapons, the consequences of exposure are far worse for the most vulnerable in the population—the very young, the very old, the sick and the poor.

We believe there can be no truly effective response to many potential uses of either chemical or biological weapons.

George Fisher, **New Internationalist,** December 1989

Fifth, a complete and total ban would provide the strongest political foundation for sanctions—economic, political, and if justified as last resort, military—either against holdout countries seeking to acquire chemical weapons or in response to their actual use of chemical weapons.

Containing the Risks of a Complete and Total Ban

Assuming continued pursuit of a complete and total chemical weapons ban, measures can also be taken now and in the future to contain its risks for U.S. security.

Several different safeguards—from continued support for chemical weapons defense and protective measures to continued commitment of intelligence resources to monitor chemical weapons potential—might be undertaken as part of eventual adherence. These would hedge against illegal activities.

Parallel U.S.-Soviet confidence building measures might be agreed upon to set limits on permitted defensive exercises that could be used to hide illegal offensive preparations. Such measures would be consistent with other confidence building measures now being negotiated in Europe.

On a bilateral U.S.-Soviet basis, additional verification commitments to supplement those in the multilateral chemical weapons treaty also could be negotiated. This would help to enhance confidence in Soviet adherence.

121

Consultations with the Soviet Union and U.S. allies also are warranted now on how to bring into a complete and total ban the key target countries in the Third World. Their adherence would be essential to realize fully its benefits.

Next Steps

In parallel with intensified activity on the negotiations front, other steps should be taken to counter chemical weapons proliferation in the Third World before a complete and total ban is concluded.

Multilateral export controls can buy time, and on-going efforts to buttress them warrant strong support. However, continuing high-level U.S. political intervention is likely to be needed to overcome bureaucratic, industrial, and foreign policy opposition overseas to tough controls. The types of sanctions legislation now under consideration in Congress against firms assisting other countries to acquire chemical weapons capabilities also would make those firms think twice before engaging in questionable deals.

More broadly, it is not too soon to initiate discussions with other countries to work out informal private understandings about what to do the next time chemical weapons are used. Public warning by other governments about the costs of chemical weapons use could be sought. Our goal must be to avoid a repetition of Iraq's extensive and unpunished use of these weapons. Passage of proposed Senate legislation to make chemical weapons users pay a price also would send an important signal to other countries.

The key to successful long-term efforts to control the proliferation of chemical weapons, in my view, remains in the conclusion of the complete and total chemical weapons ban now under negotiation in Geneva. Other non-proliferation measures can buy time, but even those measures would gain considerably from a chemical weapons ban.

18 HALTING THE SPREAD OF CHEMICAL WEAPONS

A CHEMICAL WARFARE BAN IS DANGEROUS

Frank J. Gaffney, Jr.

Frank J. Gaffney, Jr. is Director of The Center for Security Policy, a Washington D.C.-based research firm. In the following reading, Mr. Gaffney outlines his viewpoint on the risks and dangers of a total ban on chemical weapons.

Points to Consider:

1. How does the Libyan "lesson" highlight the author's viewpoint?

2. Why does the author feel a total ban is futile? Give specific examples.

3. What are the difficulties of compliance and verification?

Excerpted from testimony by Frank J. Gaffney, Jr. before the Senate Committee on Governmental Affairs, May 17, 1989.

I do not believe the United States can prevent Libya— or other nations so disposed—from obtaining the capability to manufacture chemical weapons through an arms control agreement.

Late in 1987, the United States finally resumed the production of chemical munitions, clearing the way to replace the existing inventory on a less then one-for-one basis. As a consequence, we have begun to restore to the U.S. arsenal the single, proven deterrent to chemical aggression—a reliable and effective chemical retaliatory capability.

The good judgment of President Reagan in requesting this capability, and that of the Congress in ultimately approving it, is now clearer than ever. Today a growing number of Third World nations are obtaining the means to produce and use lethal chemical agents—the subject of these hearings.

The Lesson of Libya

The much publicized Libyan chemical weapons plant at Rabta is but the most recent—if among the most frightening—of the emerging Chemical Weapons (CW) programs in developing countries. While Qaddafi's potential to employ toxic chemical weapons in pursuit of his own aggressive aims (or on behalf of the international terrorists he supports) is grounds for ample concern, at least as troubling should be what the Rabta facility suggests about CW proliferation more broadly suggests.

- First, this plant illustrates the point that there is simply no certain way to distinguish between legitimate facilities producing a range of chemical products for civilian use (e.g., fertilizers, pesticides, pharmaceuticals, etc.) and those producing weapons. The catastrophe at Bhopal, India, reveals just how lethal can be the products of some such facilities—even when used for civilian purposes.

- Consequently, the industrialized world's companies, banks and, yes, even governments are—knowingly or not—fostering the spread throughout the developing world of indigenous infrastructures with the inherent capability to produce chemical weapons.

- Even if one were able to determine on a given day—or, for that matter, over a period of time—that a plant was engaged in the manufacture of commercial chemical

124

products, there is no known means of ensuring that its equipment will not be put on CW-related uses shortly thereafter.

- Even in the absence of a treaty banning production of chemical weapons—it is excruciatingly difficult to get international agreement that a given activity is related to chemical weapons manufacture. We must expect that, should a treaty outlawing chemical weapons ever be achieved, persuading others that a given country (the Soviet Union, for example) is violating the agreement will become still more difficult.

Facts of Life

These considerations serve to make two points: First, chemical weapons proliferation is a fact of international life. Such weapons can be manufactured cheaply; there is neither a need for expensive, dedicated facilities (as with nuclear weapons plants) nor for great technical sophistication. Countries around the world are availing themselves of the ability — actual or potential — to produce lethal chemical agents.

The reasons for their doing so are diverse: some regard it as the easiest route to obtaining weapons of mass destruction — the poor man's atom bomb.

Then there is the somewhat special case of a nation like Libya. Its purpose in acquiring a chemical weapons manufacturing capability appears motivated, at least in part, by the desire to add CW to the gruesome tools of the trade of the world-wide terrorist groups it sponsors.

A second point is that the aforementioned factors make any effort to respond to CW proliferation by negotiating a ban on the production and stockpiling of chemical weapons dangerously futile. It is simply not possible today to prevent countries with modern commercial chemical industries from also having thereby the ability to produce chemical weapons. There is no verification system known today or in prospect that will be able unfailingly to detect legal chemical agent production and storage.

What is more, as the technology for manufacturing chemical products advances, the few signatures that today do provide important indication of CW activity are likely to disappear. Devices are already available on the commercial market that can manufacture legal chemical agents (and, for that matter, toxin and biological weapons) without specialized or dedicated facilities. In fact, such agents can, with this technology, be

126

produced virtually anywhere. There is no practicable verification scheme for dealing with such technical developments.

Dangerous Position

Instead of putting aside the illusion of such a CW ban, the United States is today moving forward inexorably—in part thanks to the new impetus provided by the recent international conference in Paris—toward its negotiation. In fact, anything that will emerge from the Geneva negotiations is unlikely to be either "global" or "verifiable".

A less than "global" ban: As it may well prove impossible to get every nation to subscribe to the ban, the U.S. position is that the United States will enroll so long as some substantial number of other countries (e.g., sixty) do so. On the face of it, this means that America could enter into an agreement requiring it to eliminate all of its CW capability while many other nations are under no such obligation.

A less than "verifiable" ban: As a practical matter, there is no such thing as a verifiable ban on chemical weapons. In any arms control agreement involving closed, totalitarian societies, there is always some degree of verification uncertainty. What invariably occurs is a two-step process that erodes the value of any agreement reached:

First, the negotiators establish the degree of intrusive inspections and other monitoring arrangements that every signatory can accept. Inevitably, this outcome falls far short of what is required to verify even less daunting arms control agreements than a global CW ban.

Next comes the overselling of the treaty's verification provisions. Executive branch officials troop to the Senate to attest to the verifiability of provisions they know to be deficient in important respects. They rationalize that, as long as the treaty can be "effectively," or "sufficiently" or "adequately" or "reasonably" verified, that is enough. In the end, they are betting that a party to the treaty will not cheat.

Compliance and Non-compliance

Regrettably, as the recent Paris conference illustrated so well, there is no reason whatsoever for believing that collective enforcement of compliance will occur. Indeed, the conferees found themselves unable even to mention countries (such as Iraq) clearly guilty of violating the existing international arms control agreement on chemical weapons—the 1925 Geneva convention banning their first use.

It is hard to imagine that the nations of the world will be more willing to take punitive measures when the result of a violation is not the wholesale murder of innocent civilians, brutally documented by television, but simply the existence of a building suspected of manufacturing illegal agents.

Forget About Banning Chemical Weapons

For these reasons, I strongly recommend to the Committee and the Subcommittee that you regard the Bush Administration's pursuit of a global, verifiable ban on chemical weapons with great skepticism. The President must be encouraged to abandon this potentially dangerous goal.

Ironically, those in the Administration responsible for fulfilling President Bush's oft-stated commitment to such a ban know better. Some senior officials have privately expressed their view that the ban is ill-advised; their hope is that, eventually, they will be able to disabuse the President of this illusion. In the meantime—at least in the absence of vigorous Congressional scrutiny—these officials appear unwilling to admit that the "emperor has no clothes." As a result, the United States lurches inexorably onward toward a dangerous, unverifiable chemical weapons ban.

I believe the United States cannot afford to engage in such hypocrisy. It is irresponsible to pay lip service to an objective whose accomplishment we know would be highly dangerous. American participation in a chemical weapons ban is—and will under all foreseeable circumstances remain—simply a formula for unilateral U.S. chemical disarmament.

Pursue Other Measures

This is not to say that we are unable to take—or should refrain from taking—steps to slow the proliferation of chemical weapons. I strongly support economic sanctions as a means of imposing real penalties on those who would sell or buy CW-related capabilities.

Obviously, if the United States hopes to prevail upon the other advanced industrial nations to give up lucrative sales of CW-related materials to developing nations, we must observe a consistent standard ourselves. On that point, I hope that the Bush Administration and the Congress will act to reverse an ill-considered decision taken in the last days of the Reagan Administration. This decision would permit two American firms, Honeywell and Baily Controls, to provide the Soviet Union with the technology and equipment to manufacture under joint ventures automated controls that lend themselves to more efficient CW (and nuclear) weapons production.

Maintain the U.S. CW Deterrent

In the end, however, I do not believe the United States can prevent Libya—or other nations so disposed—from obtaining the capability to manufacture chemical weapons through an arms control agreement. The effect of such an accord may be to slow proliferation marginally or—more likely—to make evidence of proliferation harder to come by. What it will assuredly do, however, is to prevent the United States from retaining the ability to deter chemical attacks against it and its allies by threatening credible, in-kind retaliation.

Based upon my thirteen years of professional experience in this field, starting with my service to this Committee, I must tell you such an outcome would entail unacceptable risks for U.S. national security and should be avoided at all costs. Unless and until a better, more reliable approach to preventing the use of chemical weapons against U.S. and allied personnel can be found, I believe the United States must maintain its own, modest but effective chemical retaliatory capability.

HALTING THE SPREAD OF CHEMICAL WEAPONS

AN INTERNATIONAL AUTHORITY TO LIMIT CHEMICAL WEAPONS

Raymond Cohen and Robin Ranger

Raymond Cohen and Robin Ranger write for the U.S. Institute of Peace, an independent institution established by Congress to strengthen the nation's capacity to promote peaceful resolution of international conflicts. This reading is taken from their paper entitled "An International Authority to Limit Chemical Weapons".

Points to Consider:

1. How would the ICWA insure the safety of a nation being attacked by an aggressor with chemical weapons?

2. What would be the primary benefits of an ICWA?

3. How would the proposed Authority be better than relying on verification and compliance?

Excerpted from testimony by Raymond Cohen and Robin Ranger before the Senate Committee on Governmental Affairs, May 17, 1989.

In return for a commitment to refrain from acquiring chemical weapons, non-CW states joining the scheme would be assured of various benefits .

An urgent challenge for the Bush administration is to produce an effective U.S. policy for halting the proliferation and use of chemical weapons (CW). Despite the best efforts of American policy-makers, the U.S. has failed to stop Iraq from using CW (including nerve gas) against Iran and the Kurds, and Libya from building its Rabta CW plant, with West German and Japanese help. The recent Paris Conference of signatories of the 1925 Geneva Protocol refrained from imposing any penalties on Iraq for flagrantly violating the Protocol's ban on the first use of CW. The Conference also saw Arab states ominously linking their acceptance of the ban on CW possession under negotiation at Geneva to Israel's surrender of its nuclear weapons.

Under these circumstances the Executive and the Legislature must quickly find answers to two questions: First, how can existing and possible future limits on CW be enforced? Second, since a universal ban on CW manufacture is now unlikely to be achieved in the near future, what immediate international agreements can be reached on limiting CW?

A constructive answer to both questions would be for the U.S. to propose the establishment, by governments committed to limiting CW, of an International Chemical Weapons Authority (ICWA). An ICWA would facilitate the imposition of penalties on states violating the Geneva Protocol and the provision of assistance to the victims of illegal CW use. The Authority would also limit CW proliferation by helping to identify both the suppliers and buyers of potential CW materials, so that such sales could be blocked.

Insurance Strategy

At the heart of the ICWA concept is the strategy of insurance. In return for a commitment to refrain from acquiring chemical weapons, non-CW states joining the scheme would be assured of various benefits: In the event of a CW attack, confirmed by an automatic, independent investigation of the UN Secretary-General:

- The victim would be supplied with all necessary defensive supplies including antidotes, suiting and gas masks, and decontamination equipment. Teams of experts would be

sent out at short notice to train the victim in their use.

- Fully equipped field hospitals and medical teams would also be rushed to the spot.

- Observers would be dispatched, with suitable publicity, to vulnerable centers of civilian population, to deter CW attack.

- Compensation would be provided to the victim. This would include financial aid, diplomatic support and military aid to balance any advantage which the CW user might have obtained by its use.

- For the first time since 1925, sanctions would be imposed on the government violating the Geneva Protocol.

RAISING THE RISKS

The potential violators of arms control agreements are a very small group indeed. Treaties such as the chemical weapons convention must seek to deter these countries by raising the risks of detection, and hence of global condemnation, as high as possible.

Elisa D. Harris, **San Diego Union**, Feb. 5, 1989

The strategy of insurance would meet U.S. objectives in controlling CW. It would provide nations with an incentive to renounce CW. It would deny potential CW users from obtaining any decisive benefit—they would be able to catch their victim off guard only once. Finally, it would actively deter the use of CW. A potential CW user would face not only the prospect of negative sanctions working to his direct detriment but also positive sanctions, working to the actual benefit of his opponent, who would enjoy the sympathy and support of ICWA.

Benefits of ICWA

But why, it will be objected, do we need yet another international agency? What would be gained by a formal body that could not be more readily obtained by informal contact or within the framework of the United Nations?

An ICWA would indeed build on the work of the informal 19-member Australian Group of governments in limiting CW proliferation by monitoring the spread of CW-making equipment and precursors, and harmonizing export controls. But a more formal body with a permanent secretariat would permit greater continuity and improve procedures for the distribution of information. Nor would members be able to ignore its findings, as West Germany and Japan ignored U.S. warnings in the Rabta case.

Moreover, by facilitating multilateral action by like-minded governments to limit CW, an ICWA would reduce the current burden the U.S. bears of being the chief enforcer of CW limits.

ICWA could also be an important test case of Soviet-American and East-West cooperation in the area of arms control. Under Gorbachev the USSR has indicated an unprecedented interest in controlling the spread of CW. This has emerged in bilateral contacts, at the disarmament talks in Geneva and most recently at the Paris Conference. The Soviet Union has also displayed noteworthy restraint in declining to supply CW manufacturing capabilities to clients such as Libya and Syria.

Within the framework of an ICWA of like-minded states, then, collaboration would be relatively insulated from the kind of political complications inherent in broader forums such as the UN. Dissenting parties opposed to CW limits would be unable to disrupt the constructive work of the organization, though they could hardly ignore its practical effects. Functional bodies, underpinned by common interest, tend to generate habits of cooperation not achievable elsewhere. Once an ICWA were in place, a positive momentum of practical cooperation might be generated with useful implications not only for the control of CW but also for East-West relations and other areas of arms control.

An ICWA would also remedy the fatal flaw in the draft Convention banning CW manufacture and stockpiling: the lack of any provisions to enforce compliance with its limits. This flaw makes the CW Convention's controversial verification provisions essentially irrelevant, because they could be violated with impunity.

An International Chemical Weapons Authority would thus be an effective means of achieving U.S. arms control objectives. In the short term, the Authority would facilitate U.S. collaboration with like-minded governments to reverse the rapid erosion of existing limits on CW proliferation and use. In the longer term, the Authority could similarly facilitate the enforcement of any future limits on CW, if these were achieved. Most important, it would provide Third World states, tempted — or alarmed — by the Iraqi precedent, with a realistic alternative to going it alone.

HALTING THE SPREAD OF CHEMICAL WEAPONS

A POLICY OF DETERRENCE IS THE ANSWER

Thomas A. Dine

Thomas A. Dine is the Executive Director for the American-Israeli Public Affairs Committee.

Points to Consider:

1. What reasons are given by the author for Israel's need for a chemical weapons deterrence?

2. In light of the recent war in the Persian Gulf, how do you feel the author's viewpoint will be affected?

3. Compare and contrast this reading with Reading 19. How do the authors agree/disagree?

Excerpted from testimony presented by Thomas A. Dine before the U.S. Senate Committee on Foreign Relations, May 9, 1989.

In the face of this dangerous situation, Israel's policy toward the use of chemical weapons is one of deterrence.

In recent years, a number of developments have taken place in the Middle East that threaten Israel's security and have justly moved the chemical weapons issue to the top of America's and the world's agenda.

First, several Arab states in the region – Egypt, Iraq, Iran, Libya and Syria – have developed the capability, aided by West European industrial firms, to wage chemical warfare. Apparently, their stocks of chemicals are sufficiently large so as to cause massive casualties if used against unprotected civilians in Israel's major population centers. Iraq, for example, is thought to be operating five chemical complexes that are capable of producing 50 tons of Tabun and Sarin nerve gas and 720 tons of mustard gas per year, while Libya is putting the finishing touches on a chemical weapons facility that will be capable of producing five tons of mustard gas daily.

Second, a number of these Arab nations have sought and are developing ballistic missile technology that will allow them to deliver their chemical warheads directly on Israeli territory. Using ballistic missiles armed with chemical warheads, Iraq showed in its recent war with Iran how inaccurate but destructive these two technologies in combination can be. Given that there is at present no effective defense against missiles armed with chemical warheads, military planners in states considering using this capability are able to contemplate a high probability of causing great death and destruction. And given that these weapons are inaccurate, unrecallable terror weapons – in contrast to highly accurate counterforce systems – they seriously increase the risk of pre-emptive strikes in a crisis.

Third, in the Iran-Iraq war, by using chemical agents, Iraq breached the ban against the use of chemical weapons that has existed since World War I. In so doing, Iraq, unfortunately, suffered only minimal condemnation from the world community. As a result, the use of poison gas now seems to have legitimacy that it has not had during most of this century.

Together, these and associated other factors raise serious questions about what the spread of chemical weapons might mean for the security interests of Israel as well as those of the

United States. Chemical weapons could be used against Israeli airbases and mobilization centers in the opening phases of an Arab offensive during a future conflict. And it would require only a few attacks with chemically-armed missiles to bring about a high number of civilian casualties. While Egypt possessed chemical weapons during the 1973 Middle East war, it opted not to employ them. Today, however, following the Iran-Iraq War and the spread of these new technologies around the Middle East, the situation might well be different in the event of hostilities. Certainly, the calculus regarding the costs and benefits stemming from their use by Arab states may well have changed in the minds of military planners in light of recent developments.

Israeli Policy

In the face of this dangerous situation, Israel's policy toward the use of chemical weapons is one of deterrence. The government of Israel favors a chemical weapons-free zone in the Middle East and has made clear on a number of occasions that any use of chemical weapons against Israel would inflict the most serious consequences upon the perpetrator. At the same time, Israel has taken a variety of measures to defend itself from the dangers posed by chemical weapons in the hands of its enemies. Its intelligence community has stepped up the monitoring of Arab production capabilities. Israel has been forced to implement a comprehensive civil defense program to defend its population against chemical attack. Gas masks and other protective gear have been stockpiled and training is offered to the general public on the steps to be taken in the event of a chemical weapons attack. Further, a range of initiatives have been instituted at military facilities such as airbases so that operations can be sustained in a chemical environment. Finally, and perhaps most significantly, the United States and Israel have embarked on a joint research project to develop an anti-tactical ballistic missile system. The so-called Arrow ATBM project, which has been underway for about a year, justly commands broad bipartisan support in the Congress. While still in the research and development stage, this joint ATBM project may prove to be a model for countries wishing to defend themselves against missiles with chemical warheads.

U.S. Policy

Given the growing threat from the spread of chemical weapons to American and Israeli interests, it is not surprising that both the U.S. Executive and Legislative branches have turned their attention to the problem in recent days. To his credit, George Bush highlighted the importance of this issue during the recent presidential campaign when he repeatedly made chemical weapons his highest arms control priority.

Since taking office, President Bush has usefully pursued this issue on several fronts. He has attempted to tighten our export control procedures regarding chemicals. He has supported active U.S. participation in the Australia Group, the 19-member grouping formed to try to control the spread of chemical weapons and the 7-nation Missile Technology Control Regime designed to stop the export of technologies that aid the building of surface-to-surface missiles. Finally, the United States has continued to pursue multilateral negotiations in Geneva to conclude a Chemical Weapons Convention aimed at prohibiting the development, production, possession and transfer of chemical weapons.

While these and other administration efforts are useful steps, more must be done on an urgent basis. For with every passing day, civilians in Israel and elsewhere are increasingly threatened by the spread of chemical weapons and possible attack, either by terrorists or by belligerent states. Accordingly, Congressional initiatives designed to prevent the spread and possible use of chemical weapons are critical.

Without analyzing here the pros and cons of all the different legislative initiatives recently introduced regarding chemical weapons, I believe that the United States ought to take the lead by enacting new legislation now to deal with this growing threat. Among other things, such legislation should:

1) Provide mandatory sanctions against nations that use chemical weapons;

2) Provide mandatory sanctions against companies and other suppliers of materials and technology which aid the proliferation of chemical weapons;

3) Broaden and tighten export controls on chemicals;

4) Encourage bilateral U.S.-Soviet efforts to control chemical weapons proliferation; and

5) Spur international efforts to control the spread of chemical weapons and ballistic missile technology.

WHAT IS EDITORIAL BIAS?

This activity may be used as an individualized study guide for students in libraries and resource centers or as a discussion catalyst in small group and classroom discussions.

The capacity to recognize an author's point of view is an essential reading skill. The skill to read with insight and understanding involves the ability to detect different kinds of opinions or bias. **Sex bias, race bias, ethnocentric bias, political bias and religious bias** are five basic kinds of opinions expressed in editorials and all literature that attempts to persuade. They are briefly defined in the glossary below.

Glossary of Terms for Reading Skills

Sex Bias—the expression of dislike for and/or feeling of superiority over the opposite sex or a particular sexual minority

Race Bias—the expression of dislike for and/or feeling of superiority over a racial group

Ethnocentric Bias—the expression of a belief that one's own group, race, religion, culture or nation is superior. Ethnocentric persons judge others by their own standards and values.

Political Bias—the expression of political opinions and attitudes about domestic or foreign affairs

Religious Bias—the expression of a religious belief or attitude

Guidelines

1. From the readings in Chapter Five, locate five sentences that provide examples of editorial opinion or bias.

2. Write down each of the above sentences and determine what kind of bias each sentence represents. Is it *sex bias, race bias, ethnocentric bias, political bias or religious bias?*

BIBLIOGRAPHY

GENERAL

Beckett, Brian. Weapons of Tomorrow. *Plenum Press,* 1983: 160 pp. il.

Bennet, J. Beyond Hijacking. *The Washington Monthly*, June, 1990: 22:24-5.

Federation of American Scientists. *Chemical Weapons Convention bulletin.* (Published Quarterly).

Kestin, H. "They May Not Be Weapons at All" (untested binaries). *Forbes,* Sept. 18, 1989: 144:45-6.

Kleber, Brooks E. The Chemical Warfare Service-Chemicals in Combat. *Office of the Chief of Military History, Dept. of the Army,* 1966:697 pp. il.

Moon, J. E. Van C. Chemical Warfare: A Forgotten Lesson. *The Bulletin of the Atomic Scientists,* Aug. 1989: 45:40-3.

Pillar, Charles. Gene Wars: military control over the new genetic technologies. New York: *Beech Tree Books*, 1988: 302 pp. il.

Robinson, Julian Perry. Chemical warfare arms control: A framework for considering policy alternatives. *Stockholm International Peace Research Institute,* 1986.

Salholz, E. Defense: a chemical reaction. *Newsweek,* April 1990: 115:25. il.

Thatcher, Gary. Poison on the wind. *Christian Science Monitor,* Dec. 13-16, 1988: 4-part series.

U.S. Department of Defense. Soviet chemical weapons threat. *Government Printing Office.*

Yamamoto, K. R. Retargeting research on biological weapons. *Technology Review,* Aug/Sept. 1989: 92:23-4. il.

DISPOSAL

Beardsley, T. Easier said than done [U.S. Army plans to incinerate chemical stockpile]. *Scientific American,* Sept. 1990: 263:48+.

Friedersdorf, M. L. Chemical weapons disposal program. *Department of State Bulletin,* June 1989: 89: 19-21.

Kemper, V. Deadly debris. *Common Cause Magazine,* July/Aug 1990: 16:20-5. il (map).

Laurin, F. Scandinavia's underwater time bomb. *The Bulletin of the Atomic Scientists,* March 1991: 47:10-15. il.

Shulman,, S. Bomb burning in the Pacific. *Technology Review,* Oct. 1990: 93: 18-20. il.

EXPORT-IMPORT/SAFETY MEASURES

Hughes, D. USAF may speed production of new suits to protect crews from chemical weapons. *Aviation Week & Space Technology,* Aug. 20, 1990: 133:27-8.

Iraqi chemical weapons development program relied on West-European assistance.

Marshall, E. U.S. bio-defenses faulted by G.A.O. *Science,* Feb. 1, 1991: 251-514.

More German dealing in the poison trade. *Newsweek,* July 10, 1989: 114-28.

Nadler E., and Windrem R. Deadly contagion [U.S. exports to Iraq]. *The New Republic,* Feb. 4, 1991: 204:18+.

Warner, M. G. and Waldrop, T. Bonn finally comes clean. *Newsweek,* Jan. 23, 1989: 113-32. il.

Weber, B. Desert wrap [protective tank covers for use during chemical attack]. *The New York Times Magazine,* Sept. 23, 1990: p.98. il.

INTERNATIONAL ASPECTS

Bierman, J. Chemical disarmament: the superpowers propose major arms cutback. *Maclean's,* Oct. 9, 1989: 102:26.

Conference on Disarmament continues work on chemical weapons accord. *U.N. Chronicle,* June 1990: 27:30-1.

Gutman, W. E. A poison in every cauldron. *Omni* (New York, N.Y.), Feb. 1991: 13:42-46. il (map)

Holmes, H. A. Biological weapons proliferation. *Department of State Bulletin,* July 1989: 89: 43-5.

Isaacs, J. D. 20-year battle on chemical weapons is over. *The Bulletin of the Atomic Scientists,* July/Aug. 1990: 46:3-4. il.

Kemper, V. Having his stockpile and destroying it too [Bush administration contradictory stance]. *Common Cause Magazine,* July/Aug. 1990: 16:23.

Whiteside, T. The yellow-rain complex [theory of M. Meselson]. *The New Yorker,* Feb. 11, 18, 1991: 66:38-42 and 66:44-68.

EUROPE

Campbell, C. and Matthews, R. The dregs of the cold war. *World Press Review,* Sept. 1990: 37:16-17.

Cohen, Raymond and Ranger, R. Breathing Room. *The New Republic,* Feb. 27, 1989: 200:8-9.

Turning off the gas [global verifiable ban]. *Commonweal,* Oct. 20, 1989: 116:548-9.

Isaacs, J. D. Mother knows best. . .But is anyone listening? *The Bulletin of the Atomic Scientists,* Apr. 1989: 45:3-4. il.

The New Face of War. *World Press Review,* Mar. 1989: 36:11-14. il.

Paris conference calls for complete ban on chemical weapons. *UN Chronicle,* June 1989: 26:58-9.

Smolowe, J. The search for a poison antidote [Paris Conferences]. *Time,* Jan. 16, 1989: 133:22. il.

LIBYA

Bierman, J. Gunning for Quaddafi. *Macleans,* Jan. 16, 1989: 102:18-19. il.

Lief, L. The uphill fight to contain chemical weapons. *U.S. News & World Report,* Jan. 9, 1989: 106:42. il.

Manegold, C. S. In pursuit of poison: Libya's chemical war plant is in production. *Newsweek*, Mar. 19, 1990: 115:33. il.

Magnuson, E. Chemical reaction [U.S. fighters down Libyan MIGs]. *Time*, Jan. 16, 1989: 133:18-21. il

The new merchants of death [West German link to Libyan weapons]. *World Press Review*, Mar. 1989: 36:13-14.

A Singed Son of the Desert. *US News and World Report*, Mar. 26, 1990: 108:14.

State Department. Libya's chemical weapons plant. *Dept. of State Bulletin*, Mar. 1989: 89-71.

Templeman, J. and Lee, D. How Quadaffi built his deadly chemical plant. *Business Week*, Jan. 23, 1989: p. 50-1. il.

MIDDLE EAST

From Baltimore to Baghdad [Alcolac Inc. ships poison gas chemicals to Iraq]. *U.S. News & World Report*, June 4, 1990: 108:51, il.

Fears of bio-warfare. *Newsweek*, Aug. 27, 1990: 116:4. il.

Gomez, E. M. Remembering an Iranian tragedy [attack on Halabja]. *Art News*, Jan. 1991: 90:70.

O'Keefe, I. Flanders Fields revisited [poison gas attacks against the Kurds]. *World Press Review*, Mar. 1989: 36:12-13.

Revkin, A. C. The poor man's atomic bomb. *Discover*, Jan. 1989: 10:76. il.

Turque, B. The specter of Iraq's poison gas. *Newsweek*, Aug. 20, 1990: 116:26. il.

MAGELLAN AND
THE RADAR MAPPING
OF VENUS

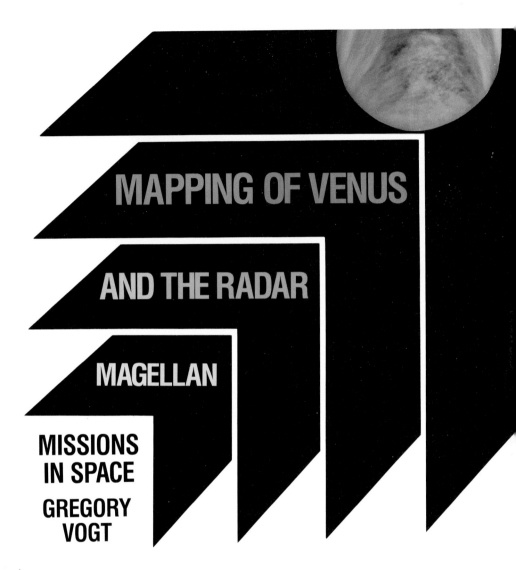

MAPPING OF VENUS

AND THE RADAR

MAGELLAN

MISSIONS IN SPACE

GREGORY VOGT

THE MILLBROOK PRESS

BROOKFIELD, CONNECTICUT

Cover photographs courtesy of NASA

Photographs courtesy of Bettmann Archive: pp. 13, 23 (top); Culver
Pictures: p. 23 (bottom); the National Astronomy and Ionosphere Center:
p. 28 (The Arecibo Observatory is part of the NAIC, which is operated
by Cornell University under a cooperative agreement with the National
Science Foundation.); Sovfoto: p. 36. All other photographs courtesy of
NASA.

Library of Congress Cataloging-in-Publication Data

Vogt, Gregory.
Magellan and the radar mapping of Venus / by Gregory Vogt.
p.   cm.—(Missions in space)

Includes bibliographical references and index.
Summary: Describes the mission of Magellan, the interplanetary
spacecraft designed to permit detailed radar mapping of the surface
of Venus.
ISBN 1-56294-146-1
1. Venus (Planet)—Exploration—Juvenile literature.   2. Magellan
(Spacecraft)—Juvenile literature.   3. Radar astronomy—Juvenile
literature.   [1. Magellan (Spacecraft)   2. Venus (Planet)—
Exploration.   3. Radar astronomy.]   I. Title.   II. Series: Vogt,
Gregory. Missions in space.
QB621.V64   1992
523.4'2—dc20   91-23494   CIP   AC

With much appreciation, I dedicate this book to William D. Nixon, a dear friend and NASA mentor who, by his example and encouragement, helped me to grow.

CONTENTS

MAGELLAN AND THE RADAR MAPPING OF VENUS

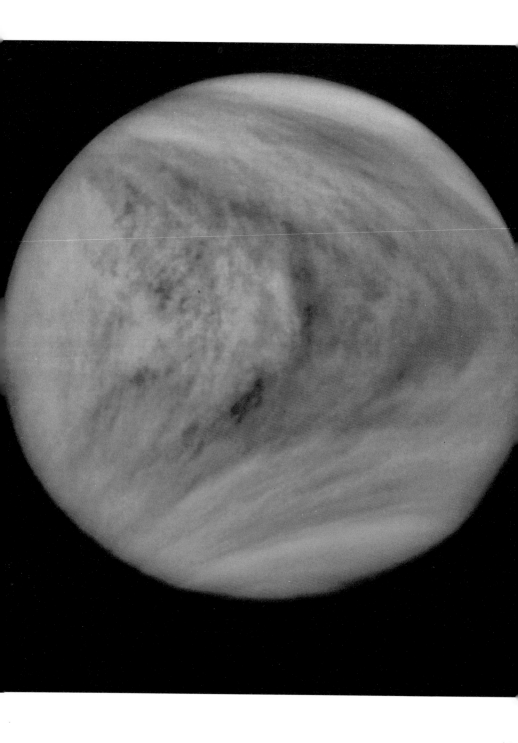

INTRODUCTION

It would be hard to imagine a world less hospitable to life than the planet Venus. Far beneath a perpetual shroud of dense, yellowish clouds lies its rocky, tortured surface. The temperature there is so high—about 900 degrees Fahrenheit—that it never gets completely dark. Even when the Sun has set, the rocks themselves glow dull red from the blistering heat they have absorbed.

Venus's atmosphere is so dense that if a human could set foot on the planet, every square inch of that person's body would be compressed by a crushing 1,300 pounds — 90 times the weight of air at the surface of the Earth. The atmospheric pressure on the surface of Venus is the same as would be encountered 3,000 feet under the ocean on Earth! Even worse, Venus's atmosphere is made almost entirely of carbon dioxide gas, and its upper layers contain sulfuric acid droplets. Carbon dioxide is one of the gases we exhale in breathing. In large concentrations, it is poisonous to humans.

Venus will probably never rate high on the list of the most popular tourists stops, even when vacation trips through the Solar System become common. However, it is high on the list of planets that astronomers want to know more about. They see it as a great mystery to be solved. The second planet out from the Sun, Venus is our nearest neighbor after the Moon. It is just a little smaller than Earth. The densities of the two planets are also very similar. Density is a measure of how much matter is packed into an object. An average cubic yard of Earth weighs 3,275 pounds. A similar yard of Venus weighs 3,086 pounds. Because of these similarities, Venus used to be described by some as Earth's twin. This characterization was always somewhat shaky, however, since until recently no astronomer had ever seen images of the planet's surface. Venus is continually covered by dense clouds that have not parted even once since the Italian astronomer Galileo pointed the first astronomical telescope at the planet almost four centuries ago. Until just a few decades ago, astronomers had to guess what lay beneath the clouds.

What did they guess its surface was like? Some speculated that Venus, being closer to the Sun than the Earth is, had to be hotter than the Earth. This could mean it was covered with jungles and swamps and had stiflingly high humidity that condensed into clouds, leading to a perpetual rain. Others suggested that Venus was

covered with foul-smelling petroleum seas that polluted the atmosphere and created a perpetual smog. Still others thought that Venus might be wracked by intense volcanic eruptions that spewed ash and noxious gases into the sky.

With the coming of the space age, Venus's true character began to be revealed. On October 4, 1957, the Soviet Union successfully launched the first satellite into Earth orbit. By the end of January 1958, the United States had become the second nation to orbit a satellite, and the two nations quickly became locked in a race to explore space. In just a few years, the first Russian cosmonauts orbited the Earth, and they were followed into space by the first American astronauts.

The early accomplishments of the U.S. manned space program gained the world's attention and overshadowed an equally important event. In 1962, less than five years after the first satellite launch, the first successful interplanetary spacecraft, *Mariner 2,* flew past Venus. The spacecraft traveled millions of miles through space and passed by Venus at a distance of 21,000 miles from its cloudtops. *Mariner 2*'s instruments gave astronomers their first close-up indications of the kind of world Venus really is.

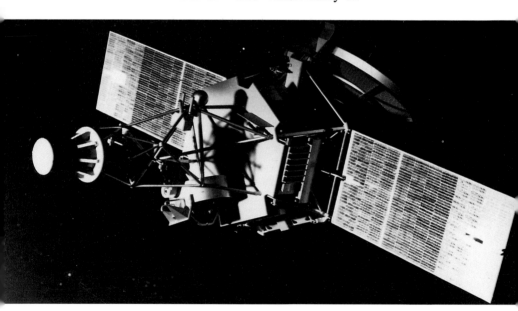

An early *Mariner* spacecraft.

Mariner 2's flight past Venus was the first of a long string of space voyages to study the veiled planet. Some spacecraft, such as *Mariner 2*, had only a short encounter with Venus. Later, landers were sent to the planet's surface, balloons were dropped into its atmosphere, and other spacecraft went into orbit around it. In all, 20 spacecraft were sent to Venus between 1962 and 1986.

In 1990, a new spacecraft arrived at Venus, and it maneuvered itself into an elliptical (egg-shaped) orbit. This spacecraft, called *Magellan*, was sent by the U.S. National Aeronautics and Space Administration (NASA) to continue our exploration of Venus and learn what the planet's surface is really like.

Magellan arrived on August 10, 1990, and began its long-term studies of Venus. A small braking rocket on the spacecraft slowed it in its interplanetary course so that Venus's gravity could capture it and pull it into orbit. After its capture, *Magellan* used powerful radar waves to penetrate the clouds and map much of the planet's surface.

NASA sent *Magellan* to Venus because astronomers wanted to learn more about the planet. Solving mysteries is what astronomers try to do. Each discovery they make helps them to understand the story of how our Solar System came into being and, more important, how life came to be.

There is a more practical side to the scientists' interest in Venus. Because it is the nearest and perhaps the most similar planet to Earth, under-

An artist's depiction of the *Magellan* spacecraft, still attached to the Inertial Upper Stage (IUS) rocket.

standing Venus could be important in predicting the future of Earth. Why is Venus's environment so harsh? Was its climate ever like Earth's? If so, what caused it to change? Could the Earth become like Venus? A solid knowledge of the natural processes at work on Venus could help us to preserve and protect the Earth for many generations to come. The *Magellan* spacecraft is still making major discoveries about this relatively unknown world. Under *Magellan*'s watchful radar eye, Venus has begun to reveal its startling face.

CHAPTER ONE
VENUS AND
THE EARLY SPACE
EXPLORERS

On the morning of May 4, 1989, a small white van rolled up to space shuttle launch pad 39B at the Kennedy Space Center in Florida. Five astronauts, wearing orange launch suits and white helmets, climbed into an elevator that took them high above the concrete launch pad and the massive steel platform that supported the space shuttle *Atlantis*. After walking across a catwalk on the access arm, they entered a small white room pressed up against *Atlantis*'s entry hatch. Each, in turn, boarded *Atlantis* and was positioned and strapped into his or her launch seat by technicians. In the drivers' seats were Commander David M. Walker and Pilot Ronald J. Grabe. In the passenger seats were mission specialists Mary L. Cleave, Norman E. Thagard, and Mark C. Lee. *Atlantis*'s entry hatch was sealed and checked for leaks, and the access arm and white room were swung away.

This was not the first time the crew of space shuttle mission STS-30 had boarded *Atlantis*. They were also on board on April 28, when they got as close as 31 seconds to lift-off before an automatic computer monitoring system shut down the launch. Sensors had determined that a hydrogen pump had developed an electrical short. The launch was "scrubbed," and the disappointed crew had to leave the orbiter. The problem took several days to fix, and the next launch attempt was not until May 4. But on that morning a launch looked unlikely. This time, weather was getting in the way. The sky was overcast, and strong winds blew, making a launch risky. Still, launch preparations continued normally. Luck was with *Atlantis* this time, because by early afternoon, with only five minutes left in the "launch window," the winds died down and the clouds parted. The launch could proceed.

At 2:47 P.M. Eastern Daylight Time, *Atlantis*'s two solid-rocket motors and three main engines fired into life. *Atlantis* climbed off the pad, leaving behind a pillar of white smoke. It headed for a 184-mile-high orbit around the Earth.

All space shuttle missions are important, but the STS-30 mission was special. It was the first time an orbiter carried a spacecraft on board destined to travel to another planet. All previous interplanetary spacecraft had been launched with unmanned rockets. The Venus-bound spacecraft in *Atlantis* was named *Magellan,* after the famous Portuguese sailor Ferdinand Magellan, whose ship circumnavigated the Earth early in the 1500s.

The space shuttle
Atlantis is launched
on May 4, 1989,
with the *Magellan*
spacecraft aboard.

FERDINAND MAGELLAN

The *Magellan* mission is named for Ferdinand Magellan, who was born in northern Portugal around the year 1480. Magellan lived during the period of great ocean exploration voyages. Famous sailors such as Christopher Columbus, Vasco da Gama, and Amerigo Vespucci were making their historic voyages while Ferdinand was still a boy.

As a young man, Magellan became a mariner himself by joining the Portuguese navy. He served in India and Asia. By the time he was 30, Magellan rose to the rank of captain and had become one of the best navigators of his day.

Eventually, Magellan renounced his loyalty to the ungrateful Portuguese king and left for Spain, where Charles V agreed to provide Magellan with the money he needed for a voyage. The purpose of this voyage was to find a new route to the Spice Islands by sailing westward, rather than eastward (as was usual), around the southern tip of Africa. The trip would take Magellan completely around the world—something that had never been done before.

On September 20, 1519, Magellan led a fleet of five ships and 265 men out of the harbor of Sanlúcar de Barrameda. After crossing the Atlantic Ocean and rounding the tip of South America, they entered a broad expanse of water that took them almost four months to cross. By chance, no storms were encountered during the passage, and they named the water the Pacific Ocean. *Pacific* means "peaceful."

Although the ocean was peaceful, the voyage was troubled. Supplies began to run low, and 19 sailors died from sickness or starvation. Finally, on March 6, 1521, land was sighted. They had reached what is known today as the Philippines. Here tragedy befell Magellan. He was killed when he got in the middle of two warring Philippine tribes.

Although Magellan did not complete the circumnavigation of the globe himself, one of his five ships, the *Victoria,* with a crew of 18 men, did. They returned to Spain in 1522. The expedition was basically a failure. Traveling east to the Spice Islands was much faster and easier. However, by traveling around the world, Magellan's ship proved what Columbus believed but could not demonstrate in his voyages—that the world is round. If you set sail and keep on going, you'll eventually come back to where you started.

Portuguese navigator
Ferdinand Magellan
(1480–1521).

Magellan's ship,
the *Victoria*, which
sailed completely
around the world.

During its fifth orbit of the Earth, *Atlantis* was repositioned to launch its payload. The 7,604-pound *Magellan* was packed in the payload bay. A platform at its far end tilted upward to an angle of 52 degrees. At the proper moment, springs popped the spacecraft and its attached booster rocket free, and *Magellan* moved out of the bay. The booster was a 32,500-pound two-stage solid-rocket motor called the inertial upper stage (IUS). Sixty minutes later, with *Atlantis* a safe distance away, the first stage of the booster was fired, and *Magellan* was on its way. *Magellan* broke free of gravity and headed toward Venus on a voyage that would take 463 days.

THE FIRST MISSIONS TO VENUS *Magellan* is just the latest of more than 20 spacecraft to travel to Venus. Venus has been studied by more spacecraft than any other planet in our Solar System except, of course, Earth. In spite of this interest, we know less about Venus than we do about the much more distant planets Jupiter and Saturn. Venus's permanent thick cloud cover makes visual study of its surface by telescopes impossible. To make progress in the study of Venus, spacecraft were an absolute necessity. Furthermore, because Venus is relatively close to Earth, it is the easiest planet to visit. At its closest point to Earth, Venus is only 26 million miles away. Mars, the next nearest planet, is nearly 50 million miles away when its orbit brings it nearest to Earth.

Study of Venus began with the ancient astronomers, who mapped the motions of all the planets

Magellan and the IUS are released
from the space shuttle's cargo bay
in the early evening of May 4, 1989.

they could see with their naked eyes. When Galileo pointed his first telescope skyward at Venus in 1610, he made a startling discovery about the planet. Venus displayed phases, like those exhibited by the Moon! Knowing that light from Venus, like light from the Moon, was really reflected light from the Sun, Galileo sought to explain why Venus went through phases. The only possible explanation he could come up with was that Venus orbited the Sun. It was an important discovery that helped verify the Sun-centered theory of the Solar System that had been put forth by the Polish clergyman Nicolaus Copernicus years before. This discovery revolutionized humankind's view of the Solar System and proved that the Earth is not at the center of the universe.

From the time of Galileo until early in the 1960s, little could be learned about Venus except that its clouds never parted. Astronomers were frustrated but not defeated. They took advantage of a discovery that was made in the 1940s. During World War II, radar was employed to detect the approach of enemy planes. A radar transmitter sends radio waves up into the sky. When the waves strike an airplane or another object, they bounce back to a radar receiver and make the presence of the object known—even in the dark or through clouds.

In the 1960s radar facilities at spacecraft tracking stations in Goldstone, California; Haystack, Massachusetts; and Arecibo, Puerto Rico, each directed powerful radar waves at Venus. Moving

Like the Moon, Venus goes through phases.
Shown here is Venus in its crescent phase.

The Arecibo radar telescope.

at tremendous speeds, the waves shot straight through Earth's atmosphere and traveled across millions of miles of space to penetrate the clouds of Venus. Radar waves striking high spots on the planet's surface bounced back toward Earth first; those that struck low spots followed. Waiting receivers on Earth captured the reflected waves and used their different arrival times to create primitive maps of Venus's surface.

These maps showed few details, but they were a start, and they permitted astronomers to make some important findings. With repeated studies, astronomers identified some features on Venus that they could recognize each time radar waves bounced off. Sometimes the features showed up and other times they didn't. This indicated that Venus rotated on an axis. The rotation rate was shown to be very slow. It takes Venus 243 Earth days to spin once on its axis. It was also concluded that Venus rotates in the opposite direction from Earth. In other words, the Sun over Venus doesn't rise in the east, as it does on Earth, but in the west.

In 1962, astronomers were presented with a new tool to study Venus. That year, NASA launched the *Mariner 2* spacecraft, which passed to within 21,000 miles of the planet's cloudtops. Spacecraft sensors measured the planet's surface temperature and determined it was very hot— about 900 degrees Fahrenheit. *Mariner 2* also discovered that the atmospheric pressure at the surface is 90 times that on Earth and that the atmosphere of Venus has poisonous concentrations of carbon dioxide gas! A magnetometer on the spacecraft failed to detect any magnetic field for the planet.

Five years passed before the next successful trip to Venus. This time, the Soviet Union sent a spacecraft. *Venera 4* not only traveled to Venus but also actually dove into its atmosphere. *Venera 4* radioed back atmospheric measurements of Venus for 93 minutes. Then, 15 miles above the surface, the pressure of the dense atmosphere crushed the spacecraft and silenced its radio.

Just one day after *Venera 4* entered Venus's atmosphere, NASA's *Mariner 5* made a flyby mission of Venus and passed to within 2,500 miles of the cloudtops. Its instruments made atmospheric measurements and confirmed the high temperature measured by *Mariner 2*. The spacecraft determined that Venus was uniformly warm. Its day and night sides had the same temperature. *Mariner 5*, like *Venera 4*, detected large amounts of carbon dioxide gas and only traces of water vapor in the atmosphere.

The next four Venus missions, spanning the years 1969 through 1973, were all Soviet. *Venera 5* through *Venera 8* one by one entered Venus's atmosphere and descended to the planet's surface. *Venera 5* and *Venera 6* descended by parachute and conducted some atmospheric studies before hitting the surface. Measurements radioed back again indicated high concentrations of carbon dioxide but no signs of water vapor. *Venera 7* and *Venera 8* also used parachutes to make soft landings on Venus. Both transmitted surface

This view of Venus, seen by *Mariner 10*'s cameras on February 6, 1974, was taken from about 450,000 miles away.

temperature and pressure readings for about half an hour before failing in the intense heat and pressure. *Venera 8*'s instruments indicated that the planet's surface resembled granite, a rock that on Earth forms from the cooling of molten lava beneath the planet's surface. The spacecraft also determined that, despite the dense cloud cover, significant amounts of sunlight still penetrate all the way through to Venus's surface.

NASA got back into the Venus business again in 1973 with the *Mariner 10* spacecraft flyby. After its encounter with Venus, *Mariner 10* went on to Mercury and made the first spacecraft visit to that planet ever. As it flew by Venus, *Mariner 10* learned that the planet is much rounder than

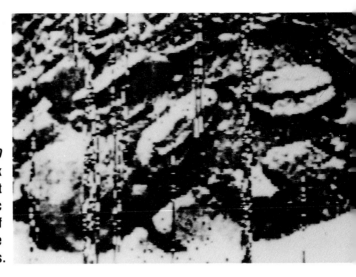

Venera 9 sent back the first panoramic views of the surface of Venus.

Earth and that the upper cloud layer resembles Earth's puffy cirrus clouds.

Not quite two years later, the Soviets were back with *Venera 9* and *Venera 10*. These lander spacecraft carried cameras and sent back the first panoramic (wide) views of Venus's surface. The pictures, though of poor quality, showed the surface to be rocky. *Venera 9* landed on a steep hill that Soviet scientists speculated could be one side of a volcanic cone. Several rounded stones that resembled volcanic bombs (frozen globs of lava blasted out during volcanic eruptions) were present. *Venera 10* landed on a level plain. The rocks beneath it seemed to be porous (full of holes) and weathered. Several deep fissures (cracks) were spotted as well. *Venera 10* broke the endurance record on Venus's surface by working for 65 minutes before the planet's heat and pressure "cooked" it.

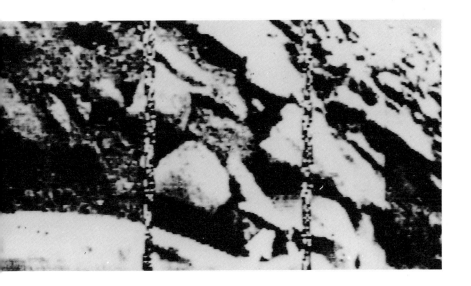

In 1978, NASA again returned to Venus, this time with a two-part spacecraft. The *Pioneer Venus* mission left Earth in two separate launches. An orbiter spacecraft, *Pioneer 12*, was launched on June 5, 1978, and a probe spacecraft, *Pioneer 13*, was launched three months later, on August 8, 1978. Because of the timing of the launches and the positions of Earth and Venus, *Pioneer 13* arrived at Venus just five days after *Pioneer 12* went into orbit. *Pioneer 12* carried crude radar equipment for mapping Venus's surface. The maps revealed highlands, rift valleys, and a mountain perhaps 7 miles high. Rift valleys are long, narrow depressions in the ground. They are formed by land that has sunk due to its location between parallel faults in a planet's crust.

Pioneer 13 added to our knowledge of Venus by splitting into four probes. Each probe pene-

An artist's depiction of the *Pioneer Venus* mission.

trated the atmosphere to take pressure, wind, and temperature readings.

Eight more spacecraft were sent to Venus before the *Magellan* mission in 1990. All were sent by the Soviet Union, and all were designed as entry vehicles rather than flyby craft. *Venera 11* arrived at Venus on December 25, 1978— the same month as *Pioneer 12* and *Pioneer 13*. A lander descended to the surface. Meanwhile, a flyby spacecraft relayed radio signals from the lander back to Earth.

During its descent, the lander recorded electrical activity and noise in the atmosphere. This activity indicated the possible presence of lightning or huge volcanic eruptions. *Venera 12* tried to repeat the *Venera 11* mission, but the landing craft's cameras failed to return any surface pictures. *Venera 13*, in 1982, returned the first color pictures of Venus's surface, and the *Venera 14* lander drilled into the planet to study soil samples. *Venera 15* and *Venera 16* were orbiter missions similar to NASA's *Pioneer 12*.

The Soviet Union's *Vega 1* and *Vega 2* were the last spacecraft to travel to Venus before *Magellan*. Both were launched to intercept with Halley's comet as it passed near the Sun during March 1986. However, on their way to the Halley encounter, both swung by Venus, and each dropped two spacecraft into Venus's atmosphere. Two descent vehicles dropped to the surface, while the other two vehicles entered the atmosphere and deployed balloons. These balloons enabled probes with instruments to float

The Soviet Union's *Vega* spacecraft was intended to
visit Halley's comet, but it first swung by Venus
to drop an instrument package into its atmosphere.

around in the atmosphere 33 miles above the surface. For 46 hours each probe transmitted wind, temperature, and pressure data.

The data from the many early spacecraft voyages to Venus, plus Earth-based radar and telescope observations, were assembled to form a long-awaited picture of the shrouded planet. Much remained to be learned, but the basic outline was at last clear.

Venus is the second planet from the Sun in the Solar System. At an average distance from the Sun of 67 million miles, it receives almost twice as much sunlight as does the Earth. Its orbit around the Sun is more nearly a circle than is that of any other planet. At a speed of nearly 22 miles per second, it takes about 225 Earth days for Venus to make it around the Sun.

Venus spins on its axis, as does the Earth, but the tilt of its axis is only 3 degrees. Earth's axis tilts 23.5 degrees. Furthermore, Venus rotates very slowly, only once every 243 days, and it does so backward relative to the Earth's spin. The backward slow spin and the planet's orbit around the Sun combine to make a year on Venus less than two Venus days long.

The diameter of Venus is 7,520 miles. This is a little more than 400 miles less than the diameter of Earth. Its surface gravity is about nine tenths that of Earth.

The clouds are Venus's most noticeable feature. If we could take a ride down to the planet's surface, the first clouds we would encounter

VENUS: EARTH'S TWIN (?)

MARS

THE INNER SOLAR SYSTEM   MERCURY   VENUS

EARTH

	Earth	Venus
MASS	1.0 $M_\oplus$	0.82 $M_\oplus$
MEAN RADIUS	6371 km	6051 km
DENSITY	5.52 gm/cm^3	5.11 gm/cm^3
ROTATION	1 DAY DIRECT	243 DAYS RETROGR/
SURFACE TEMP.	300°K (80°F)	750°K (900°F)
ATMOSPHERE	1 BAR PRESSURE	92 BAR PRESSURE
	NITROGEN, OXYGEN	CARBON DIOXIDE

would be at an altitude of just over 40 miles. The tops of those clouds are yellowish-white. This is because, instead of being made of water vapor or ice crystals, as clouds on Earth are, these clouds are made of sulfuric acid droplets.

The ride through this first cloud layer would be rough. Our wind-speed instruments tell us that the wind speed is nearly 225 miles per hour (mph). If we were to descend no further, we would be swept completely around the planet in only four days. Other instruments register an outside temperature at this altitude of minus 45 degrees Fahrenheit.

Continuing downward to about 34 miles above the planet's surface, we come to a second cloud layer. This time, the clouds are composed of tiny solid particles that we can't identify. They are mixed with a fine mist of acid droplets raining down from above. The temperature has now climbed to a balmy 60°F. The wind speed has dropped to about 100 mph. At 31 miles, the temperature has picked up considerably, to over 160 degrees, and our imaginary spacecraft passes through a third cloud deck. The temperature keeps on climbing.

The atmosphere begins clearing at 30 miles up. But here the temperature is close to the boiling point of water. Lots of chemical activity is taking place, as sulfuric acid and the solid particles start breaking down into molecules of water, the gas sulfur dioxide, and even oxygen. The lightest of these molecules float upward on the heavier, denser ones, where they recombine back into acids to rain down again in a continuing "acid rain" cycle.

It has become very noisy outside our imaginary spacecraft. Lightning flashes continuously. Without the insulation of the spacecraft's walls, the constant booming and rumbling of the storms around us could make us go deaf. The wind has continued to diminish. As we try to make out details of the landscape below, everything looks blurry. The carbon dioxide atmosphere is becoming denser, and the view is something like what a goldfish must see when looking outside its glass bowl.

At 20 miles above the planet's surface the temperature is a blistering 430 degrees Fahrenheit. The closer we get to the surface, the higher the temperature and the pressure become, but the slower the wind speed. We finally touch down on a hard, rocky surface. The temperature is 850 degrees. The atmospheric pressure is 90 times greater than Earth's at sea level, and the wind speed is a mere 2.5 mph. However, because the air is so dense, a slow breeze on Venus has all the force of a strong river current on Earth.

Outside the window of our imaginary spacecraft, we see a weird rocky world that glows red from the sunlight filtering through the clouds above. We have landed on one of three continent-sized landmasses. They are not really continents, because Venus is much too hot to have oceans surrounding the continents. But if Venus did have real continents, this landmass would stick up high enough to be one. Called Aphrodite Terra, this region is about the size of South America. It is located along the planet's equator. A second landmass is called Ishtar Terra, and it is near what would be Venus's arctic circle if the planet had a polar ice cap. Ishtar Terra is roughly the size of Australia. The smallest landmass, called Beta Regio, could be a volcanic shield. It covers an area about the size of the Hawaiian Islands on Earth. (Volcanic shields on Earth are very broad and gently sloping volcanic cones.)

An artist's conception of Venus's surface,
based on *Pioneer Venus* data.

Shown here is an artist's conception of the Venusian landform known as Ishtar Terra, a continent-sized mass about the size of the continental United States.

If we were to move our spacecraft around the planet's surface, we would come to many different land forms among the broad plains, lowlands, and highlands. The plains of Venus could be considered equivalent to sea level on Earth; all altitudes are measured above or below this level. The rolling plains cover about 65 percent of the planet and have an average altitude of 3,750 miles from Venus's center. They wrap completely around the planet. In several places,

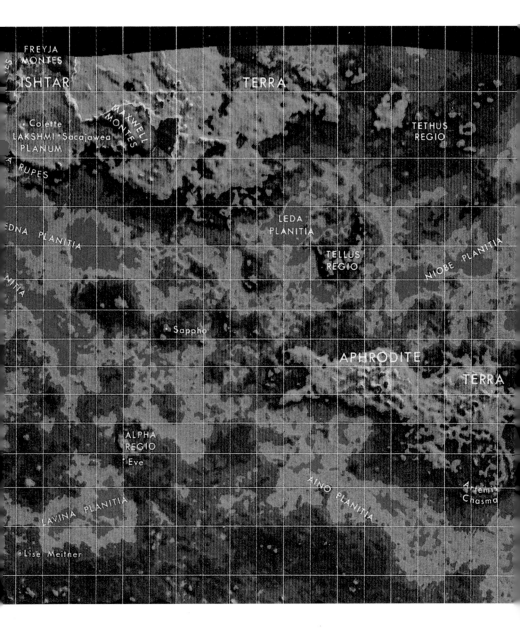

A topographic map of Venus. Blue areas represent Venusian lowlands; highlands are shown in green, yellow, and red.

covering about 16 percent of the planet's total surface, the land drops steeply beneath the plains by as much as 9,000 feet. If there were water on Venus, these would be the ocean basins. The remainder of the planet consists of highlands. The highlands feature some of the most dramatic terrain, including mountains taller than Mount Everest, steep escarpments (large cliff faces), canyons, and circular craters that may be of volcanic origin.

Our imaginary ride to the surface of Venus has been somewhat sketchy in its details. This is because the details were based on the explorations of the 20 space missions to Venus that took place between 1962 and 1986. Some details, such as temperature, pressure, wind speed, and atmospheric composition, were fairly accurate, but the description of the nature and shape of the surface itself was less certain.

The Soviet landers that took pictures were limited by how far their cameras could see. Radar mapping by *Mariner 10* gave us a broad view of the surface, but it could not obtain any fine detail. At best, its radar system could make out surface objects 31 miles across or wider. This allowed for detecting really large mountains, canyons, and continent-sized masses, but not smaller features. It gave us a general picture of Venus's surface, but a general picture permits us to make only general conclusions. For example, although scientists could state with some certainty that there were large mountains on Venus, they could not say much about how those mountains evolved. Did they form as the result of volcanic action—large masses of land pushing against one another and mounding up in the middle—or as the result of land pulling apart? A detailed explanation of Venus's surface could be based only on a detailed view, one that might be possible with the next mission to Venus— *Magellan.*

CHAPTER TWO
THE *MAGELLAN* SPACECRAFT

Before *Magellan* there was the *Venus Orbital Imaging Radar* mission—*VOIR* for short. Early in the 1970s, when spacecraft explorations of Venus were still in their infancy, scientists at NASA's Jet Propulsion Laboratory (JPL) in Pasadena, California, began designing a large spacecraft to explore the second planet. The *VOIR* mission was intended to map Venus with radar and to conduct many scientific investigations from orbit. Unfortunately, the plans for the spacecraft became too elaborate, and the price tag became too high. In 1982, the year after the space shuttle began flying, *VOIR* was canceled.

Though JPL scientists were deeply disappointed, they refused to give up. They went back to their drawing boards and almost completely redesigned the spacecraft. They gave it a new name as well—the *Venus Radar Mapper*. This name was eventually changed to *Magellan*.

The 1978 *Pioneer Venus* mission had tantalized scientists by providing them with exciting but crude radar maps of volcanic mountains, canyons, continent-sized plateaus, rolling plains, and basins. But missing from the maps was the detail. The new spacecraft, *Magellan,* would be able to see objects as small as 800 feet across.

Part of the reason that the original *VOIR* mission was so expensive was that everything about its design was new, and many of its parts had to be built from scratch. Custom parts are expensive. To save money, spare parts built for other spacecraft, such as the *Voyager* probes, would be used on *Magellan* whenever possible. Some parts could even be used for several purposes. For example, instead of having separate antennae for radar mapping and communications with Earth, *Magellan*'s primary antenna could serve both purposes. Designing the craft with only one science instrument, the radar sensor, proved another big cost savings. And still another was placing *Magellan* into an elliptical (egg-shaped) orbit around Venus instead of a circular one. To slow *Magellan* down from its trip across space so that Venus's gravity could capture it and send it into orbit, rockets would have to be fired. To put the spacecraft into an elliptical orbit would take less rocket thrust than would putting it into a circular orbit. Less thrust means a smaller rocket, which would cost less.

The *Magellan* craft itself soon began to take shape. It would have a total weight of 7,604

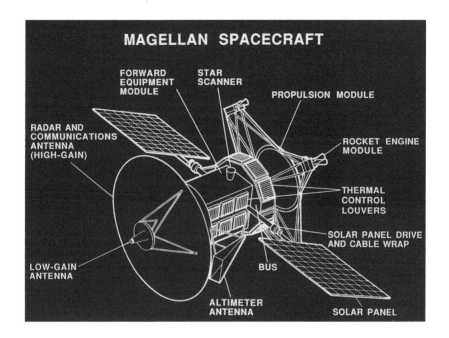

MAGELLAN SPACECRAFT

FORWARD EQUIPMENT MODULE

STAR SCANNER

PROPULSION MODULE

RADAR AND COMMUNICATIONS ANTENNA (HIGH-GAIN)

ROCKET ENGINE MODULE

THERMAL CONTROL LOUVERS

SOLAR PANEL DRIVE AND CABLE WRAP

LOW-GAIN ANTENNA

BUS

ALTIMETER ANTENNA

SOLAR PANEL

pounds. Its length would be 21 feet. In addition, two solar panels, when stretched out from the sides, would extend *Magellan*'s total width to 32.8 feet.

The spacecraft would consist of several antennae, several structures to hold equipment, a propulsion module made up of attitude (direction) control rockets plus a braking rocket to put the craft into orbit, and the solar panels. For its launch, two additional rocket motors would be added to *Magellan*. These would get the spacecraft to Venus after it was released in orbit by the space shuttle. The rocket motors would increase the total length of the spacecraft by another 17 feet and its weight by another 32,500 pounds. However, only the actual *Magellan* spacecraft and its braking rocket would arrive at Venus. The rocket motors for launch would separate from the spacecraft when their job was done.

MAGELLAN'S RADAR Radar is an invisible form of radiation, just as ultraviolet light, X rays, and radio waves are. Radar is similar to the microwaves that are used to cook food in a microwave oven. Certain forms of radar waves can penetrate through air and clouds. That is why radar was chosen for use on *Magellan*.

Radar waves are emitted by a transmitter and travel outward like ripples on a pond until they bounce off something. Some of what is reflected returns to the transmitter, where it is received by a dish antenna. Usually, the transmitter and the receiver are contained in one antenna. The bowl shape of the dish antenna concentrates the returning waves something like the way a magnifying glass concentrates sunlight to burn paper. As with the magnifying glass, the bigger the antenna, the more energy it can concentrate.

From the returning radar waves, the radar operator can determine many things about the object that reflected the waves. When radar is used at airports, the operator will know the altitude, speed, and direction of an airplane and can even estimate the plane's size by the strength of the returning waves.

Radar systems work in a manner similar to the way sound travels through the air. If you were blindfolded and led into various rooms, you could estimate the size of the rooms just by the way sounds carried in them. We cannot hear echoes in small rooms, but we can in larger rooms, such as gymnasiums. To determine the distance to the object reflecting radar waves, we measure how long the waves took to travel to the object and return. The longer the trip, the further away the object. The direction from the radar transmitter to the object is determined by noting the direction from which the reflected waves came. If the direction of the reflected waves keeps changing, that means that the object is moving.

Using radar to make detailed maps of Venus would require a very large antenna. The larger the antenna, the more detailed the map. Unfortunately, big antennae are expensive to build and even more expensive to launch. Just packing them inside of a space shuttle is a tough problem. *Magellan* spacecraft planners decided instead to use a small antenna and a trick called synthetic aperture radar, or SAR. As one of their cost-cutting measures, they would pull a spare *Voyager* spacecraft antenna off the shelf and use it on *Magellan*. It was a dish-shaped antenna 12 feet across. (A dish's diameter is referred to as its aperture.)

SAR would take advantage of the spacecraft's motion. Since *Magellan* would be orbiting Venus once every few hours and would not be sitting still, each pulse of radar would be released in a different place. It would be received in still

Magellan aims its primary antenna at Venus
to collect data during a mapping pass.

another place. Because *Magellan* would move in the time between the release and the return of the pulses, the antenna would act as if it were much bigger than it really was.

The received radar waves would be converted into data and radioed to Earth to be fed into a computer. The computer would be programmed to process the data as though it had been sent from a very large, stationary spacecraft antenna instead of a smaller, moving one. In other words, the computer could "synthesize" a larger aperture antenna and hence the name of the system— synthetic aperture radar.

As the spacecraft orbited Venus and began its mapping, the SAR would emit several thousand radar pulses every second. The pulses would flash down toward the planet and reflect off the surface. The antenna would always be aimed off to the left side, and its radar waves would bounce over a 16-mile-wide path stretching 10,000 miles long. The area covered would reach from the planet's north pole to about 70 degrees south latitude. The south pole would be missed because of the inclination of the spacecraft's orbit.

Magellan would be in a nearly polar orbit. Actually, the angle made by the orbit and Venus's equator (the orbit's inclination) would be about 85 degrees. That meant that *Magellan* would fly just to the side of the north and south poles. Because the SAR would be looking off to the left for the entire orbit, it would be looking at the north pole as it passed over but away from

Magellan's first orbit and data swath.

the south pole when it traveled to the other side of the planet. This meant, in effect, that the south pole would just be missed during mapping. From earlier radar maps of the planet, the north pole looked more interesting than the south pole. Thus, scientists considered it more important to map the north pole. However, the south pole would not be ignored entirely. If the spacecraft continued working long enough to finish mapping the northern part of the planet, its radar sensor would then be reprogrammed and aimed at the other side for mapping the south pole. As it turned out, this was exactly what happened.

After the radar waves were reflected off the planet's surface, they would be received by the antenna and stored as digital (number) data in a tape recorder system. When the spacecraft had completed a pass over a given area, its orbit would carry it to the planet's other side, where it would radio back to Earth the radar measurements it had made. By the time the tape recorder was rewound and ready to record again, the spacecraft would pass back again over the planet's other side to take new measurements. The entire procedure would take exactly one orbit. In the meantime, Venus would have rotated a small amount. Thus, the next path that the radar covered would be just to the left of the first.

Near Venus's equator, the two successive mapping paths would overlap only slightly, but near Venus's poles they would converge just as longitude lines on a world globe do. The paths would overlap a great deal there. Scientists decided they could reduce some of the duplication of data caused by this overlap by starting one path at Venus's north pole and ending it at about 70 degrees south latitude. They then would delay the start of the next path by about 5 minutes so that it started farther south but also ended farther south at 70 degrees south latitude. With this strategy, most of Venus's surface would be covered by radar maps with a minimum amount of duplication.

SPACECRAFT EQUIPMENT

Magellan would be much more than just a radar instrument. To enable the radar to work, there would have to be lots of support equipment. This would include equipment for electrical power, radio communications, data processing, heat control, propulsion, and attitude control. All this equipment, plus the radar instrument, would be stored together in three main modules: the forward equipment and propulsion modules and a third module called the equipment bus.

As its name implies, the forward equipment module would be located at the front end of the spacecraft. Here would be the large dish antenna that would be used for the radar instrument. This module also would house the radar electronics, radio, some of the attitude-control equipment, plus the spacecraft's batteries. The module would consist of a box made out of aluminum tubes with panels to cover the sides. It would be about half the size of a telephone booth. Two sides of the box would have louvers for keeping the unit cool. Louvers are similar to home heating or air conditioning vents that can be opened and closed to control the air coming from them. Temperature control would be a serious problem for *Magellan* since working electronic parts tend to get hot. Furthermore, the Sun's heat could literally cook the spacecraft. The louvers in the module walls would release excess heat to space.

On the opposite side of the forward equipment module from the dish antenna would be the ten-sided equipment bus. It, too, would be made from aluminum tubes and panels. The bus would be 6.6 feet in diameter and 17 inches thick. It would contain the spacecraft's flight computers, the connections between the computers, and the spacecraft's onboard systems, tape recorders, computer memory, and pyrotechnic control devices. With *Magellan* stowed in the space shuttle for launch, its solar panels would be folded and bolted tight to the spacecraft. After deployment from the shuttle into space, the panels would have to be unfolded. In order to do that, the bolts would have to be released. The simplest way to accomplish this would be to use pyrotechnic (exploding) bolts. An electric current would be sent to the bolts, causing them to explode and release the panels. The controlling circuitry for making this happen would be in the equipment bus. These same devices would also control the firing of the solid-rocket motor that would slow *Magellan* enough to allow it to go into orbit around Venus. This motor would later be jettisoned from the spacecraft by additional pyrotechnic bolts.

The propulsion module would be attached to the side of the equipment bus opposite the forward equipment module. It would be an open structure made of tubes that would hold the solid-rocket motor just described and 24 smaller thruster rockets. The smaller thrusters would be used to keep *Magellan* pointed in precisely the right direction during interplanetary travel to Venus. They would also be used for aligning the solid-rocket motor in exactly the right direction so that its firing would place *Magellan* in the right orbit around Venus. Finally, the thrusters would be used from time to time for making small corrections to *Magellan*'s orbit around Venus.

Stretching out from opposite sides of the equipment bus would be the two solar panels. Each panel would be 8.2 feet square. The panels, held away from the bus by arms that unfolded, would spread outward some 33 feet from tip to tip. To make electricity from sunlight, each panel would be partially covered with solar cells. Together, the panels would have a total output of 2,400 watts of electricity at 28 volts. Solar cells are most efficient in producing electricity when their temperature is less than 240 degrees Fahrenheit. Unfortunately, the Sun could heat *Magellan* in orbit around Venus to well over that. To keep the temperature down, the front side of each solar panel would contain narrow mirrors to reflect sunlight and lower the temperature.

Being closer to the Sun than Earth is, Venus would pose major thermal (heat) control problems for *Magellan*. Spacecraft can get very hot, but they can get very cold as well. While one side of the spacecraft is in sunlight, the opposite side is shaded, and the temperature of the shaded side can drop to minus 400 degrees Fahrenheit! Consequently, the difference in temperature from one side of the spacecraft to the other can be more than 800 degrees!

To keep the various spacecraft parts at the right temperatures, different coatings would be used. Electronic housings, such as the equipment bus, would be covered with multilayered thermal insulating blankets made of aluminized plastic, Dacron, and Astroquartz (a fabric somewhat sim-

Magellan extends its solar panels to face the Sun, collecting solar energy to make into electricity.

ilar to fiberglass cloth). The thermal blankets would have 18 layers. Added to the blankets would be thermal louvers to exhaust excess heat and more mirrors to reflect sunlight. Ironically, the thermal insulation would work so well that some spacecraft parts would tend to get too cold. To insure that the instruments sensitive to cold would not get too cold, small electrical heaters would be included and would turn on when necessary.

Another big concern was how to keep the spacecraft pointed in the proper direction at all times. When the spacecraft was mapping Venus, its big antenna would have to be pointed down very precisely toward Venus's surface. When it was sending data back to Earth, it would have to reorient itself to aim its dish antenna at Earth. During each orbit of Venus, the spacecraft would have to change its attitude (direction) four times. Since the spacecraft was designed to work for at least one Venus year (243 days), it would orbit the planet a total of 1,852 times. With four changes of attitude per orbit, over 7,400 attitude changes would have to be planned.

The traditional method of attitude control takes advantage of the scientific principle known as Newton's Third Law of Motion. This law states that for every action there is an opposite and equal reaction. To apply this principle to changing spacecraft orientation, small rocket thrusts are used. An attitude-control rocket fires, causing the spacecraft to rotate in the opposite direction from the rocket's exhaust. This works well in changing the spacecraft's orientation, but there is one problem. Because there is no friction in space to stop the spacecraft's rotation, it would continue to turn and turn. A second rocket firing is needed in the opposite direction from the first to stop the turning started by the first. In other words, for 7,400 attitude changes, *Magellan* would be required to fire the engines almost 15,000 times. This many rocket firings would mean huge fuel tanks, and there just wasn't room for these on the space shuttle.

The strategy used by *Magellan*'s designers to control spacecraft attitude takes advantage of Newton's Third Law of Motion while getting around the large fuel-tank problem. The way it works is similar to what happens when you step off a skateboard. You go one way (action) and the skateboard rolls away in the opposite direction (reaction). *Magellan* would utilize this principle with three reaction wheels. The wheels would be heavy disks, aimed in different directions, that would be spun with solar-powered electric motors. A wheel spun in one direction would start the spacecraft rotating in the opposite direction, just as the skateboard begins moving when you step off it. When the spacecraft rotated to a new direction, the motor would reverse the spin of the wheel, and this would stop the spacecraft's rotation. With three different reaction wheels, the spacecraft could rotate in any direction required.

Two more major spacecraft systems would be required for *Magellan*. One would be the command and data handling system and the other the radio. Command and data handling requires a computer system that receives commands from Earth, via radio, and distributes those commands to the various spacecraft systems. Commands include exactly when and where to reorient the spacecraft, when to turn on and off the radar, and at what temperature to keep spacecraft systems.

Commands received from Earth would be stored on a tape recorder for use at a later time. Two tape recorders would be built into the spacecraft's command and data handling system, but only one recorder would be used. The second would be used only if the first failed. In addition to storing command instructions, the tape recorder would store the radar data collected by the spacecraft. The recorder's tape could hold 1.8 gigabits of data. (A gigabit equals one billion bits of storage.) Thus, *Magellan*'s tape recorder could record nearly 2 billion bits of radar data.

With each radar pass over Venus, the tape would be filled. At the completion of the pass, the spacecraft would begin circling the other side of Venus and the tape would rewind. In the meantime, the attitude-control system would reorient the spacecraft to point the dish antenna at Earth. Computer commands would then order the tape recorder to play back its data so that it could be radioed to Earth. The radio system would be able to send data to Earth at a rate of nearly 270 kilobits per second. (A kilobit is one thousand bits.) At this rate, it would take almost two hours to send all of the tape-recorded data back to Earth from a single mapping orbit. Finally, the tape would be erased and rewound in time for the next radar pass over Venus.

CHAPTER THREE
THE VOYAGE
TO VENUS

On May 4, 1989, 42,000 pounds of rocket thrust propelled *Magellan* on its way to Venus. With the space shuttle *Atlantis* at a safe distance, the first stage of the IUS rocket, attached to *Magellan,* fired for about 150 seconds before separating and falling away. Two and one-half minutes later, the second stage fired, kicking out 18,000 pounds of thrust for nearly 110 seconds. With its job done, it too separated from *Magellan.* *Magellan* was by then speeding along on a path that would cover 788 million miles of space and reach Venus in 463 days.

Launching a spacecraft to Venus—or to any other planet—is a complicated business. Planning must take into account the relative positions of Earth and Venus in their respective orbits around the Sun. It is also necessary to consider the length of time the spacecraft will take to get to Venus so that when the trip is over, the spacecraft and Venus will be in the same place. The whole thing is rather like riding a carousel while trying to shoot at a target tossed in the air across a field a mile away. The bullet must be aimed where the target will be when the bullet arrives and not where the target is at the moment of firing. Finally, the spacecraft has to approach its target at the right speed and from the right direction. This will ensure that the firing of the spacecraft's braking rocket will cause the spacecraft to be captured by the planet's gravity and go into orbit.

A big consideration in launch planning is the power of the launch vehicle that will be used to send the spacecraft on its way. More rocket thrust means greater speed and a shorter travel time. Less thrust means a longer trip. *Magellan* was originally scheduled to be launched in April of 1988. Instead of using the IUS for its boost from the space shuttle's orbit, it was to be propelled by a much more powerful rocket stage, the Centaur. The Centaur uses liquid hydrogen and liquid oxygen for propellants, rather than solid fuel. Liquid fuels in combination are some of the most powerful rocket propellants known. With a Centaur, the trip to Venus would have taken only four months.

However, the development of the Centaur as a space shuttle upper stage was interrupted by the tragic *Challenger* disaster, in which seven astronauts, including a teacher, were killed when their space shuttle exploded during its launch in 1986. Investigators examined every aspect of the

The Inertial
Upper Stage
(IUS) rocket,
with its USA
insignia, is
mated to
the *Magellan*
spacecraft.

space shuttle program at that time. They found many things they believed could be changed to improve safety. One of the things they recommended was *not* to allow the Centaur upper-stage rocket to be carried in the space shuttle's payload bay. They believed that the hydrogen and oxygen propellants, which ignite easily and are very explosive, would constitute an unnecessary hazard. Solid-propellant rocket boosters would be safer.

Magellan mission planners went back to their drawing boards and computers. They refigured *Magellan*'s trajectory (course) using the IUS as its booster rocket. The flight to Venus would take more than four times longer than had been planned with the Centaur. To make the new trajectory work, Earth and Venus would have to be on opposite sides of the Sun from each other. *Magellan* would circle the Sun one and one-half times before arriving at Venus. During that time, Earth would make one and one-quarter orbits around the Sun, and Venus would circle just over two times.

With trajectory calculations complete, *Magellan* was ready to leave Earth orbit and head toward a rendezvous with Venus. The launch was perfect, except for a faulty solar panel that refused to lock into its extended position. Spacecraft controllers used a little trick to fix the problem. They rolled the spacecraft into a new position. When the acceleration from the IUS came, the thrust helped to get the panel to lock. It was similar to the way a car door left open will close on its own when the car rolls forward.

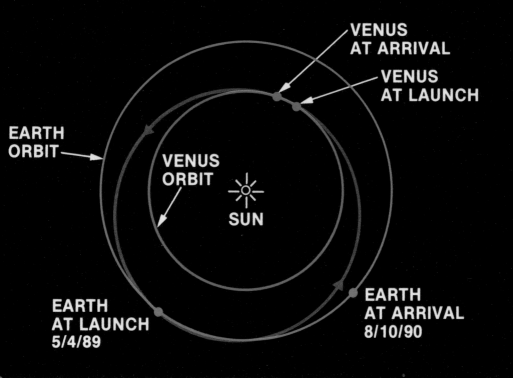

MAGELLAN TRAJECTORY

VENUS
AT ARRIVAL

VENUS
AT LAUNCH

EARTH
ORBIT

VENUS
ORBIT

SUN

EARTH
AT LAUNCH
5/4/89

EARTH
AT ARRIVAL
8/10/90

The interplanetary cruise to Venus was largely uneventful. There were, of course, the usual course corrections to fine-tune the trajectory, and there were lots of "housekeeping" chores to attend to. These included continually monitoring the spacecraft's systems and radar instrument to insure peak operating efficiency.

A few problems did arise, including faulty readings from a star sensor used to determine the spacecraft's attitude in space. Star sensors work in almost the same way you determine the direction you are facing at night by looking for the North Star. If that star is directly in front of you, you are facing north. If it is to your back, you are facing south. *Magellan*'s star sensors permit spacecraft controllers on Earth to determine which way the spacecraft is pointing and how to turn it so that its radar sensor is pointing toward Venus for mapping and toward Earth when it sends its collected data back. A faulty star sensor could have meant major problems for the mission. However, the problem was solved by sending up computer programming instructions that filtered out the faulty readings.

Another problem that arose during the trip to Venus was that some parts of the spacecraft were getting too warm. Portions of the body of the spacecraft were about 20 to 40 degrees warmer than they should have been. The problem was temporarily solved by orienting the spacecraft's large dish antenna so that it shielded the spacecraft's body from sunlight.

Magellan finally reached Venus on August 10, 1990, 463 days after it left Earth orbit. During its voyage it traveled at an average velocity (speed) of 71,000 mph with respect to the Sun. As it approached Venus, its velocity relative to the planet was 9,900 mph. (Relative velocity can be understood by comparing Venus and *Magellan* to two automobiles traveling in the same direction on a highway. One is traveling 50 mph and the other 60 mph. Consequently, the relative velocity of the faster car is only 10 mph!)

Magellan in orbit around Venus, its
large antenna turned toward the planet.

Venus's gravity pulled on the incoming craft and accelerated its speed to 24,340 mph. This was too fast. If the acceleration were permitted to continue, the spacecraft, rather than being captured by the planet's gravity, would swing by Venus and continue orbiting the Sun. *Magellan* mission planners had expected the spacecraft's increase in velocity and were ready for it. *Magellan* would have to slow itself down. At the right moment, the third solid-propellant rocket motor (the only one still attached to the spacecraft) blasted out more than 15,000 pounds of thrust as it fired for 84 seconds. The braking action of the rocket motor, seven times the force of Earth's gravity, slowed the spacecraft to 18,500 mph, and Venus's gravity caught hold of it. *Magellan* was drawn into an elliptical, near-polar orbit.

CHAPTER FOUR
THE MAPPING
BEGINS

On April 4, 1991, jubilant *Magellan* mission controllers made an important announcement. The primary goal of the *Magellan* mission, to map at least 70 percent of Venus's surface, had been accomplished more than one month early! Mission planners had expected that the spacecraft would need 243 days, the same number of days it takes Venus to rotate once on its axis, to get the job done. Instead, *Magellan* had accomplished its goal in only 201 days! Completing the primary goal early meant that by May 15, 1991—the official end of the first mapping cycle—*Magellan* had actually covered 84 percent of the planet's surface. Scientists were thrilled. The next mapping cycle, they decided, would concentrate on obtaining pictures of the remaining 16 percent of the planet's surface, including the never-before-seen south pole region.

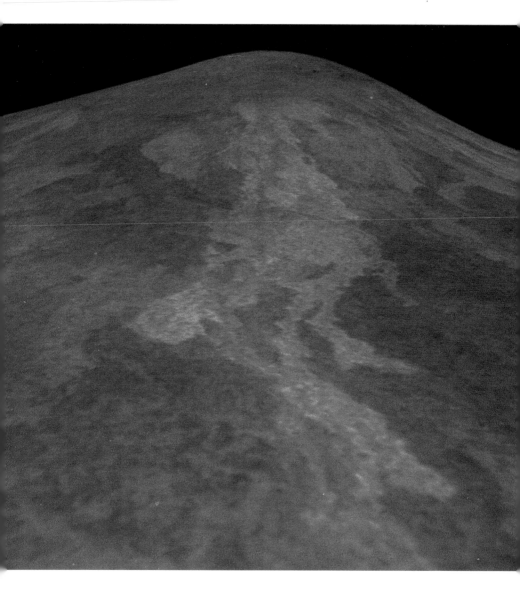

A false-color *Magellan* view of the volcano Sif
Mons, located in Venus's northern hemisphere.
The volcano is 1.2 miles high and 180 miles in
diameter. A series of bright and dark lava flows
can be seen in the center of the image.

Achieving their primary goal early had been no simple task. After entering its orbit around Venus, *Magellan* had more than its share of problems in communicating with Earth. Virtually every spacecraft has some problems affecting its operation, but these can usually be fixed while the craft is in flight or at least worked around. This was true of *Magellan* as well. Unfortunately for the *Magellan* team, problems arose when the media were still buzzing with the reported problems of another NASA spacecraft, the Hubble Space Telescope. Consequently, they pounced on *Magellan*'s problems and accused NASA of being unable to manage complex science projects. By the time the news media had moved on to other stories, both spacecraft were operating, though not exactly as planned.

One of *Magellan*'s problems occurred during its first day orbiting Venus. *Magellan*'s attitude-control computer shut down, and backup components took over the job of controlling which way the spacecraft was pointing. However, in attempting to fix the spacecraft's position, the backup components locked onto an incorrect star. Certain stars, called guide stars, can be used as celestial street signs that tell the spacecraft which way it is pointing at the moment. This allows computers to realign the spacecraft, if needed. By selecting the wrong star, the backup components caused *Magellan* to point its main antenna away from Earth. Consequently, communications with Earth were interrupted. About 15 hours later, contact was reestablished, but it was lost again the next week and then reestablished once more.

In spite of the communications problems, controllers prepared the spacecraft for its mission. On September 15, 1990, the mapping of Venus began. In spite of a tape recorder not working, which required a backup tape recorder to take over, and a few minor computer problems, the spacecraft began doing the job its builders designed it to do. *Magellan* began mapping Venus.

The almost constant stream of data that has been radioed to Earth since *Magellan*'s mapping began has excited and thrilled scientists. Venus has been shown to be an incredibly complex world. Adding the new *Magellan* data to what had already been gathered by other spacecraft missions and to radar measurements made with radio telescopes from Earth, a clearer picture of Venus has emerged. The planet has begun to reveal to us its unique personality. Although there are a number of similarities, Venus is definitely not Earth's twin.

The surface of Venus is now known to be covered by volcanic plains. It is crisscrossed with cracks and folds, which are telltale signs of past movements of the crust, or upper layers of the rock that makes up the planet. Also revealed, but to a lesser extent, were craters formed by meteorite impact and significant wind action.

THE VOLCANOES OF VENUS Perhaps the most striking new discovery concerning Venus is the extent to which volcanic activity has shaped the planet's surface. Tens of

This *Magellan* image from the Atla region of Venus shows several types of volcanic features. Lava flows coming from circular pits or linear cracks form flower-shaped patterns in several spots. A collapsed depression near the center of the image is drained by a lava channel about 25 miles long. There are also numerous surface fractures and valleys.

thousands of small volcanoes dot the Venusian plains, which cover about 65 percent of the surface of the planet.

Volcanoes and their outpourings of lava have built up a wide variety of landforms both small and large. Scientists have grouped the small volcanic features into four basic types. The great majority of these, about 90 percent, are small domes or shield cones. These are generally several hundred yards high and range from 1 to 3 miles in diameter, although some domes reach 12 miles in diameter. Shield cones on Venus appear to have resulted from outpourings of thick volcanic lava from the planet's interior. As hot lava welled up from the interior of Venus, it spread out in a circular fashion much the way pancake batter spreads out on a griddle. However, unlike pancake batter, the domes remained thicker in the middle and thinned out at the edges. Often, the shields have small craters in their centers about half a mile in diameter or less. Like shield volcanoes on Earth, these craters appear to be linked to central lava conduits, or pipes (cracks in the rock below), through which the lava traveled. The lava occasionally also formed lakes that overflowed and spread out to create the circular shield shape. After the eruption, the remaining lava in the lake drained back into the conduits, forming an easily seen circular crater in the center of the shield.

Less common on Venus are flat-topped or tablelike shields. These structures are uniformly thick except at the edges, where they drop off steeply. Another of the less common small volcanic land forms are shields that have very broad summits (peaks) and irregular slopes; some have thicker edges than centers. Also found on Venus are groups of small, cone-shaped volcanoes that form chains. These chains are found along cracks where lava was able to escape.

Much larger volcanic mountains are present on Venus as well. Hundreds of intermediate-sized (12 to 60 miles in diameter) shields have been seen, and still larger structures, over 60 miles high and up to 220 miles in diameter, have also been located. One of these larger structures, about 1 mile deep, is a caldera that was recently named Sacajawea Patera. (Calderas are large basins that form when surface rock collapses after the hot lava underneath it has flowed out.)

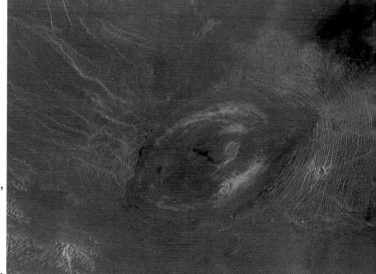

Sacajawea Patera, a large caldera that formed from volcanic activity in the Lakshmi Planum (Plain).

Sacajawea Patera is between 120 and 180 miles in diameter, about twice the size of New Jersey, and it is larger than typical calderas found on Earth or Mars.

By and large, the most common of all volcanic features on Venus are the broad expanses of lava flows, or floodings, that have accompanied the formation of volcanic shields and fissure-type eruptions. (Fissures are long cracks through which lava can pour out.) Such floodings have covered large areas of the rolling plains of Venus. Often, multiple lava flows meet and merge. Some flows measure as much as 500 miles long.

SURFACE MOVEMENTS

Although *Magellan* cannot show us Venusian quakes in action, it is obvious from images of the surface sent back by the spacecraft that quakes have been very common there. The plains of Venus show considerable evidence of the movements of large landmasses. Cracks—many of them coming together from different directions—ridges, and mountain chains are very common. In some areas, the movements appear to have compressed the land; in other areas, the land is pulling apart. Many of the cracks clearly have provided molten rock below the surface with easy routes to travel to the surface. Also, the pressure of molten material trying to escape can force pieces of the crust above to move against each other.

One of the more interesting forms of terrain on Venus is the tessera. Tesseras are broad areas where two or more sets of features, such as

The tortured surface of Venus, with its compressed
and cracked terrain, is revealed in this image of
the northeast portion of Danu Montes (Mountains),
which border on the Lakshmi Planum.

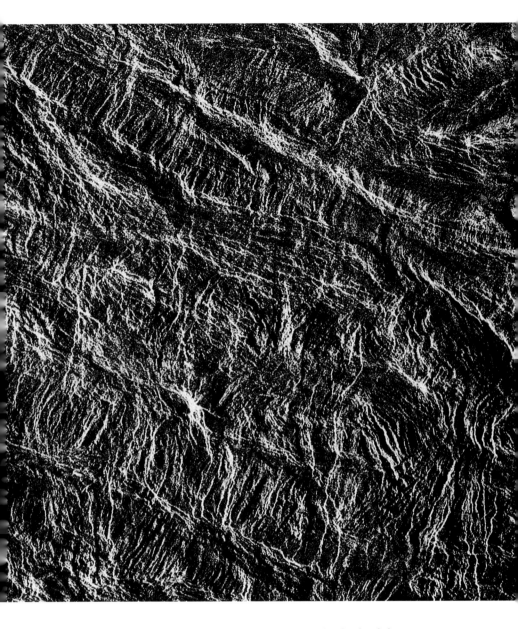

This mosaic of Alpha Regio in the Lavinia
region of Venus clearly reveals the pattern of
intersecting ridges and valleys called "tesseras."

ridges, troughs (ditches), and steep scarps (lines of cliffs), come together. Tesseras usually rise .5 to 1 mile higher than the surrounding land. They are probably the result of large compression movements of portions of Venus's crust. The result is similar to the kind of thickening produced by squeezing the ends of a fat gum eraser. As the land is compressed, it crumples and cracks to form ridges, troughs, and scarps. Tesseras can cover very broad expanses of the Venusian surface—each as much as 600 miles across.

Much higher than the tesseras are the four mountain belts girdling Venus's northern hemisphere. The elevations of some of these belts in the Ishtar Terra highlands reach nearly to the height of Mount Everest on Earth. Like tesseras, the mountain belts appear to be the result of thickening caused by compression of the planet's crust. Scientists have had some difficulty, however, explaining why the mountains are found where they are and why the crust is so thick. Some have proposed that the mountains were thrust up partly by rocky material from beneath. Other scientists feel that a better explanation comes from examining what is happening in their vicinity. The four mountain belts partially surround a not quite circular region on Ishtar Terra where there is intense volcanic activity. In this area there may be a great upwelling of heat and molten material from Venus's interior.

IMPACT CRATERS Spacecraft have shown that all rocky planets and their moons have had their surfaces modified at

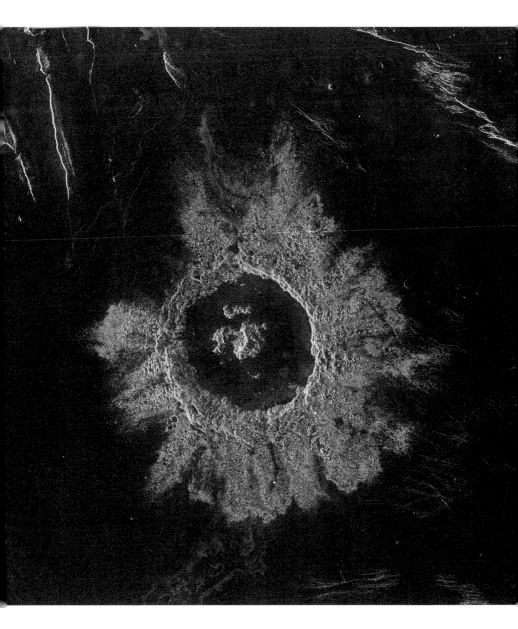

A typical impact crater showing
its surrounding ejecta blanket.

least somewhat by meteorites striking them from space. On moons and planets where there is little or no atmosphere to create friction to slow down or disintegrate meteorites on their way in, the surface is peppered with craters. Where there is a substantial atmosphere, such as on Earth, fewer meteorites make it down, and many of the craters that are formed eventually erode away through wind and water action.

Impact craters resemble the craters that are found in the center of volcanic shields. Thus, it is sometimes difficult to tell them apart. However, impact craters form from the impact of a chunk of rock that has driven itself into the surface at speeds of thousands of miles per hour. The meteorite and the rock it slams into simply disintegrate in a large explosion that leaves a hole behind. Sometimes, there is so much heat generated by the impact that the rock underneath melts briefly and sloshes about. It then rebounds back up into the center of the crater. This is similar to the sloshing that takes place when a pebble falls into a pool of water. Because molten rock is thicker than water, it moves more slowly, often allowing the rock to cool long enough to form one or more central peaks in the crater.

Impact craters also feature piles of debris scattered around the outside of the crater itself. These bits of surface rock and meteorite are called ejecta blankets.

Compared to the number of volcanic shields and cones it has found, *Magellan* has detected very few impact craters on Venus. Undoubtedly, this is largely due to the very thick Venusian atmosphere, which presents a formidable obstacle to incoming meteorites. In fact, no craters smaller than about 2 miles in diameter have been discovered. Scientists believe that meteorites likely to make smaller craters have not survived entry through the atmosphere. Only the very biggest meteorites have made it to the surface. Most craters that have been found are larger than 15 miles in diameter, and several are over 50 miles in diameter.

Generally, impact craters on Venus resemble impact craters on other planets. They have one or more central peaks, cracks in the shape of multiple rings (all with a common center), and ejecta blankets. Some craters have several floors or appear in clusters. This is thought to be due to the breakup of larger meteorites into smaller pieces, each of which hit the surface separately. Often, the ejecta blankets themselves are not spread uniformly around the crater. Ejecta blankets tend to collect on the opposite side of the crater from the direction in which the meteorite came, although wind in the atmosphere can blow the debris back.

One very unusual kind of impact has been discovered by *Magellan*. In this impact, the meteorite never actually made it to the ground. Instead, piles of rubble were created by the shock waves produced from the meteorite's collision with the atmosphere.

A "triple crater," or "crater field," was imaged by *Magellan* in September 1990.

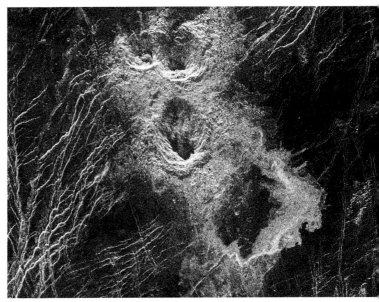

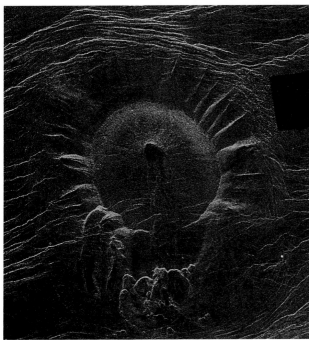

This oddly formed crater was found in the Eistla region of Venus in the southern hemisphere. (The black area in the picture indicates a data gap.)

The *Galileo* spacecraft during its construction.

BELATED MESSAGE:
GALILEO'S PEEK AT VENUS

When *Magellan* left Earth in May 1989, it headed on a course that should have made it the 21st successful spacecraft to study Venus. However, by the time it arrived in August of the next year, it was number 22. Another spacecraft had slipped in to become 21. The *Galileo* spacecraft, launched five months after *Magellan,* was sent to study Jupiter. Because of space-shuttle safety restrictions, it was also unable (like *Magellan*) to use the powerful Centaur upper stage for its launch. Instead, it had to fly a more leisurely course to the giant planet, stealing orbital energy from both Earth and Venus. *Galileo* uses the gravitational pull of the planets it approaches to pick up extra velocity. This permits the spacecraft to be launched with less powerful but safer booster rockets.

On its way to Jupiter, *Galileo* passed by Venus, on February 10, 1990. The spacecraft came to within 10,000 miles of the cloudtops of Venus. Mission scientists couldn't resist turning on *Galileo*'s science instruments for a quick peek at the planet. However, they had to wait until the middle of November before the data collected could be relayed to Earth. The reason for the delay was that the spacecraft's most powerful antenna was folded and shaded to protect it from overheating as it sailed through the inner part of the Solar System. It was not until *Galileo* used the same gravitational maneuver to pick up speed from Earth as it did with Venus that the data could be sent back to Earth. While passing close to Earth, the spacecraft was able to use its low-power antenna to radio the data collected nine months earlier. So, as it turned out, *Magellan* was still the 21st spacecraft to radio data about Venus to Earth, even though *Galileo* had collected its data months before.

Galileo added some new information to what was already known about Venus. Its instruments were designed for data collection at Jupiter, and it carried no radar instrument to map the surface. Nevertheless, it did transmit data that could be used to make pictures of Venus's atmosphere. It also provided enough data to make two atmospheric maps showing how heat energy comes up from the surface of Venus, or at least from its lower atmospheric layers. Boiling up from the planet's equatorial region on the afternoon side of the planet were heat currents that resembled the kind of atmospheric circulation accompanying huge rolling thunderhead clouds on Earth. Also found were numerous smaller hot spots. Astronomers were especially interested in the hot spots, because their presence could help determine whether volcanic eruptions were still taking place on Venus. If volcanoes on surface maps of Venus made by *Magellan* and hot spots on *Galileo*'s maps lined up, it would be a sign that the volcanoes on Venus are active and could erupt again at any time.

In other studies, *Galileo*'s magnetometer, used for measuring magnetic fields, confirmed that Venus has no detectable magnetic field. Another instrument, one that detects electrically charged particles, determined that the planet's upper atmospheric layers are able to deflect the electrically charged solar wind particles that stream out from the Sun in all directions. *Galileo* found that Venus's atmosphere divides the solar wind stream much the way the bow of a boat cuts through water.

This is a view of Earth as *Galileo* swung past it on its way to Jupiter.

WIND   Meteorite impacts are one of the forces that change the surface of Venus. Other important agents of change are wind-blown dust and sand. Many areas of Venus show long streaks of wind-blown material, and large areas of the planet are covered with blankets of sand and dust. Especially prominent in *Magellan*'s images are wind streaks that have formed on the lee (downwind) sides of meteorite craters and volcanic cones.

The wind speed on the surface of Venus is only about 1 to 2 mph. A similar wind speed on Earth would barely cause a ripple on a sandy beach. But Venus has a much denser atmosphere than does Earth, and even low wind velocities are sufficient to kick up sand and dust and move it around. Consequently, Venusian winds shape the surface of the planet and leave recognizable streaks that can be seen from orbit.

A NEW   The *Magellan* spacecraft has provided a new
VIEW OF   perspective on the second planet from the Sun.
VENUS   It has provided detail that could only be guessed at but not confirmed by previous missions. It has shown us that the surface of Venus is relatively young and that it is both similar to and very different from Earth's. Like Earth, it has highlands, plains, and deep basins. There are mountains, volcanoes, and impact craters. Like Earth, the surface has ridges and is grooved and cracked. But the surface of Venus is far more tortured. The planet is a very dynamic world, showing signs of many surface movements and volcanic eruptions. However, compared to Earth,

Unusual features called "coronae" were found to be quite common on Venus. Coronae are thought to form as a result of heat welling up from the interior of the planet and melting the crust. The molten material then rises toward the surface, causing it to dome. The dome later collapses, resulting in a ring of fractures.

most of these surface movements are small in scale. Scientists could not detect any huge continent-sized movements of Venus's crust like those that are so common on Earth. And, although there is a dense atmosphere surrounding Venus, there is no water on the surface.

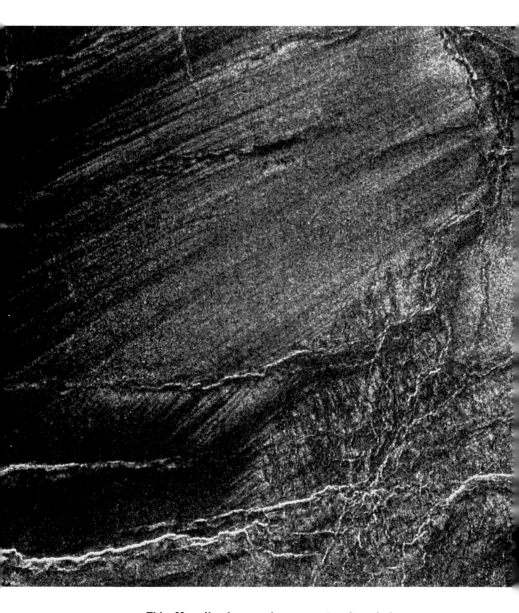

This *Magellan* image shows spectacular wind streaks near the crater named Mead. Mead is the largest impact crater known to exist on Venus.

"Pancake" domes (bottom center and left),
evidence of volcanic activity, can be
seen in the dark plains of Alpha Regio.

The absence of water is not surprising considering how hot the planet is. But there are no signs of water being present in Venus's past, either. Running water is an important agent for change on Earth. It wears down mountains and carves out wide valleys. Such features should be visible on Venus if water was present in its past. Scientists wonder why no signs of water can be detected. Earth, its nearest neighbor, is rich in water. Why not Venus?

In the absence of water, some of the most important agents for geological change on Venus are lava flows, which can flood low-lying land and cover up impact craters, and wind-blown sand and dust.

Magellan has revealed an unweathered surface on Venus. Its cracks, ridges, troughs, mountains, volcanoes, lava flows, and impact craters are all sharply defined. This has made it difficult for scientists to estimate the age of Venus's surface. Scientists use the steady rain of meteorites as a kind of impact-crater "clock" for estimating the age of a planet's surface. If there are many worn or barely visible craters mixed in with younger and sharper craters, the surface is old. If the craters are mostly sharply defined, the surface is young. Venus's craters are extremely sharp. This has led scientists to estimate the surface age to be anywhere from a few hundred million to almost one billion years old. In planetary time scales, even a billion years old is young. Scientists are asking why.

THE CONTINUING MAGELLAN MISSION

With any luck, *Magellan* should continue to function into the mid-1990s. New mapping cycles will permit maps of Venus's south pole to be made, as well as measurements of Venus's gravitational field. The gravitational field of a planet is determined by its density. The more dense a planet is (the more matter that is packed into it), the greater its gravitational field. However, planets aren't uniformly dense, and differences in surface gravity from one place to another can be measured. *Magellan* will take gravity measurements of Venus on every fourth orbit by pointing its antenna toward Earth during its mapping passes. As the spacecraft passes low over the planet, its orbit will change slightly depending upon the density of the land just beneath it. If the density increases, the gravitational pull will increase, and *Magellan* will dip closer to the planet. If the reverse is true, *Magellan* will rise slightly. The altitude changes in the spacecraft's orbit will cause subtle changes in its radio signal to Earth. This data will enable scientists to construct a gravity map of the surface of Venus that will provide important clues as to the inner workings of the planet.

As it nears the end of its useful lifespan, mission controllers hope to use *Magellan* for a unique experiment that could help future space explorers. A large part of the mass of a spacecraft like *Magellan* is the rocket engine and propellant tanks that enable it to slow its velocity and enter planetary orbit. If some of this mass could be eliminated, more and longer-lasting science instruments could be carried. One proposal for cutting the mass would be to use the atmosphere of the planet of destination to help slow the spacecraft for orbital insertion. The spacecraft would be programmed to dip into the planet's atmosphere and to use the friction generated by that activity to help slow it down.

Magellan spacecraft controllers want to try this technique with *Magellan*. By directing it to dip into the atmosphere, they hope its velocity will change enough to permit the spacecraft to alter its orbit from an ellipse to a circular shape. If it is successful, the maneuver will not only prove the technique works but also permit *Magellan* to get a closer view of the polar regions of Venus and to send back important new data.

With each new interplanetary spacecraft mission, our understanding of the Solar System changes and grows. The *Magellan* mission and all the other spacecraft that have proceeded it to Venus have had the effect of peeling away layers of paint from an old canvas to get at the original picture beneath. Much is left to be learned, and scientists will study the stream of data about Venus that continues to be sent from *Magellan* for years to come. They not only hope to learn about Venus but also hope to apply that knowledge to understand better the geological and environmental changes that take place on Earth.

GLOSSARY

Aperture. The diameter of a radar dish antenna.

Aphrodite Terra. The largest continent-sized highland landmass on Venus.

Atlantis. The space shuttle that carried the *Magellan* spacecraft into Earth orbit.

Beta Regio. The smallest of the three continent-sized highland landmasses on Venus.

Caldera. A large, circular crater formed from the collapse of a volcanic cone.

Centaur. NASA's liquid-hydrogen and liquid-oxygen upper-stage rocket.

Conduit. A pipe or vent in the ground that permits molten material to rise up to the surface.

Dome. A broad and slightly rounded volcanic cone.

Ejecta blanket. The splattering of debris around the impact site of a meteorite.

Equipment bus. The portion of the *Magellan* spacecraft that houses the spacecraft's flight computers, tape recorders, pyrotechnic control devices, and related equipment.

Forward equipment module. The portion of the *Magellan* spacecraft that supports the large radar antenna and houses the electronics for the spacecraft's radar and radio as well as other equipment.

Galileo. A NASA spacecraft that was launched five months after *Magellan* and passed near Venus on its way to Jupiter.

Impact crater. A circular depression or hole formed in a surface from the explosive impact of a meteorite.

Inertial upper stage (IUS). The two-stage solid-propellant rocket used to send *Magellan* on its interplanetary course after it was placed in Earth orbit by the space shuttle.

Ishtar Terra. A continent-sized highland landmass on Venus.

Magellan. NASA's Venus radar-mapping spacecraft.

Mariner. A series of NASA spacecraft that were launched to study Venus.

Patera. A volcanic caldera.

Pioneer Venus. A two-part NASA spacecraft mission to orbit Venus and send atmospheric probes to its surface.

Propulsion module. The part of *Magellan* containing the rocket that fired to slow the spacecraft so that it could go into orbit around Venus as well as smaller navigational rockets.

Pyrotechnic control device. A unit that sets off explosive bolts to separate, for example, the propulsion module from the *Magellan* spacecraft.

Radar. A device that determines the location of a distant object by measuring the way certain waves reflect off it.

Sacajawea Patera. A very large caldera on Venus.

Shield. A broad and slightly rounded volcanic cone.

Synthetic aperture radar (SAR). A computer technique that enables a small radar antenna to act as if it were a large one.

Tesseras. Areas of intersecting ridges, troughs, and scarps on Venus.

Vega. A series of Soviet spacecraft that dropped balloons with instruments attached into Venus's atmosphere while the craft were on their way to a rendezvous with Halley's comet.

Venera. A series of Soviet orbital and lander spacecraft sent to study Venus.

Venus Orbital Imaging Radar (VOIR). The name of an ambitious spacecraft, later canceled, that was planned for Venus observations and radar mapping.

Venus Radar Mapper. The original name of the *Magellan* mission.